D0341109

RISE
ABOVE

RISE

ABOVE

How to Go Faster, Farther, & Higher in Your Faith

JAMES RANDALL ROBISON

Inprov, Ltd.

RISE ABOVE

How to Go Faster, Farther, & Higher in Your Faith

Copyright© 2014 James Randall Robison

ISBN: 978-0-9914820-3-0

For further information, write Inprov, at:
2150 E Continental Blvd, Southlake, TX 76092

All rights reserved. No part of this publication may be reproduced, stored in a retrieval system or transmitted in any form or by any means, electronic, mechanical, photocopying, recording or otherwise, without the prior written permission of the copyrights owners.

Unless otherwise noted, Scripture references are taken from the NEW AMERICAN STANDARD BIBLE®, Copyright © 1960, 1962, 1963, 1968, 1971, 1972, 1973, 1975, 1977, 1995 by The Lockman Foundation. Used by permission.

Scripture references marked "NIV" are taken from the THE HOLY BIBLE, NEW INTERNATIONAL VERSION®, NIV® Copyright © 1973, 1978, 1984, 2011 by Biblica, Inc.® Used by permission. All rights reserved worldwide.

Scripture references marked "NLT" are taken from the Holy Bible, New Living Translation, copyright ©1996, 2004, 2007 by Tyndale House Foundation. Used by permission of Tyndale House Publishers, Inc., Carol Stream, Illinois 60188. All rights reserved.

Scriptures marked "MSG" are taken from The Message. Copyright © 1993, 1994, 1995, 1996, 2000, 2001, 2002. Used by permission of NavPress Publishing Group.

Scriptures marked "NCV" are taken from the New Century Version®. Copyright © 2005 by Thomas Nelson, Inc. Used by permission. All rights reserved.

CONTENTS

INTRODUCTION

I hate flying.

If you ask me, it defies logic. The physics of flying are both amazing and terrifying. The Boeing 777-300, like the one I recently took from Los Angeles to Hong Kong, can carry over 500 passengers. It's over 200 feet long and weighs in the range of 2.5 tons, or 550,000 pounds, when fully loaded at takeoff. In my non-engineering mind, this thing should never get off the ground. It doesn't seem natural. Birds were made to fly, not this enormous mass of metal. Yet if a highly-flammable fuel catapults it fast enough, it will rise into the air and cruise at an average of 35,000 feet above the earth. The whole idea is that if you just go fast enough, you won't fall to the ground (assuming it doesn't explode!). This sort of freaks me out.

Then there's the human element. Nobody can guarantee that the flight will arrive safely. I don't know the pilots or the crew, and no matter how skilled or well-intentioned they may be, they can't predict everything. Dozens of things can go wrong and, despite their stellar track record, they have. My wife chastises me for watching those television shows documenting airline disasters, but they fascinate me. I can carry on a conversation about the United Airlines flight that burst into flames in an Iowa cornfield, the debate around EgyptAir flight 990 that went down in the Atlantic off the coast of Massachusetts, the only fatal accident of the Concorde, and a dozen other tragic crashes. I'm a real downer for the casual, optimistic flyer.

Add to that the fact that I don't know the other passengers, who may or may not have good intentions, and commercial flight becomes a bit of a sticking point for me. The overall lack of control makes me nervous. Despite the statistically riskier prospect of driving across the country, I don't think twice when doing that. But getting on an airplane? Well, you get the point.

Still, I fly. That fact remains that I would never get to the places I want to go if I didn't. I've been to over 20 countries on four continents, so I've flown everything from Air Uganda to China Southern Airlines. I may be a white-knuckled flyer, but fear doesn't hold me back.

The same can be true with our faith.

In some ways, it defies logic – human logic, at least. We are told to lose our life in order to find it. The first are last and the least are greatest. The only savior is one who died, then came back to life. We are asked to give up control and trust someone we can't see. There's a serious strain of thinking here that isn't natural.

Then there's the human element. Many well-intentioned people, including leaders, have drifted way off track. Some have even used God for their own selfish or nefarious means. People in churches can be hypocritical, mean-spirited, and downright human. If faith depended on mankind, there's no way I'd ever get on board.

These fears, and dozens of others, can keep us stuck on the ground. We are afraid to really commit. We buy a ticket to fly, but stay in the terminal where it's safe. We wear tourist t-shirts from exotic places and pretend like we've been there. Some people never even find the airport.

The result is that we never get to the places we want to go – the places God *intends* for us to go. As believers, we are made to soar far above this earth, going places impossible to go to with our own power and doing things we never imagined. But it's not too late to take off now. A few steps in the right direction will start the journey of a lifetime.

PREPARING
FOR FLIGHT

Anyone who has ever traveled knows that the first step is not merely showing up at the airport. There are a few things that must be done before the flight takes off. The same is true spiritually. We must begin with some basic preparations in order to go on the spiritual journey God has in store for us.

Claim Your Ticket

Before you can be allowed to get on a flight, you need a ticket, and someone has to purchase it. Many people attempt to buy their own ticket to Heaven through an array of actions. Some are worthwhile, others are not.

Here's the good news: Someone already bought your ticket. In fact, there's only one who can actually pay the price, and He already did. Of course, I'm talking about Jesus Christ. His mission on earth was to redeem all of us through His death and resurrection. 1 John 2:2 says, *"And He Himself is the propitiation for our sins; and not for ours only, but also for those of the whole world."* That word *propitiation* means "to obtain the favor of." We are born outside of God's favor because we are all born sinners.[1] Through His perfect life, willing sacrifice, and triumphant resurrection, Jesus Christ gives us the gift of returning to God's favor. He is our free ticket to a new life.

This free ticket is called grace. This differs from mercy, which means you don't receive the punishment you deserve. Grace means "unmerited favor." It is one thing to avoid punishment, but quite another to receive an unimaginable reward that we don't deserve. Yet that is the offer extended to every one of us.

Christ obtained the favor of God through His sacrifice, and He then offers this favor, which we don't deserve, to us by His grace. The mercy we receive by not having to pay the price for our sins is a direct result of His grace, but it is not the entire package. His grace not only allows us entry into eternal Heaven, but enables us to have a real, vibrant relationship with God while here on earth.

Paul said, *"For by grace you have been saved through faith; and that not of yourselves, it is the gift of God; not as a result of works, so that no one may boast"* (Ephesians 2:8–9). This truth eliminates an awful lot of religious stipulations regarding salvation. There is an infinite list of things (some of them good) that people insist will make you a Christian or get you favor with God, including:
- Calling yourself a Christian
- Going to church
- Baptism

....
[1] *Romans 5:19*

- Tithing
- Speaking in tongues
- Belief in a "higher power"
- Self-realization
- Being a good person or doing good things
- "Walking down the aisle"
- Saying a prayer
- Confirmation
- Reading the Bible

For the most part, these are great things. But all of them rely on you to essentially buy your own ticket. But returning to favor with God relies on what Christ already did. If you engage in these things in an attempt to earn your salvation, you have things dangerously misplaced. You may feel better about yourself and you may even help others in the process, but you risk being one of those to whom Christ says, *"Depart from me, I never knew you"* (Matthew 7:21–23).

It's like sticking wheels where the wings should be. Yes, an airplane needs wheels to taxi down the runway, but not in place of the wings. You need a ticket to get on board, but none of these things will suffice. You cannot go to church enough, pray enough, say the right things, do the right things, or give enough time or money to earn it. Trying will only make you frustrated or self-delusional. If you begin to think you have succeeded, you will only succeed in inflating your pride.

Paul succinctly summed up this message in his letter to the Romans. First, he points out *"all have sinned and fall short of the glory of God"* (Romans 3:23).

I remember hearing about Evel Knievel when I was just a little boy. In 1974, he bought a patch of land that included a canyon on the Snake River in Idaho. He hired a Navy engineer to build him a rocket that he called a "Sky-Cycle" and tried to jump the river. He missed by a long shot and crashed 600 feet below at the edge of the river. But it wouldn't have made much difference if he had only missed by a few feet. He still would have ended up at the bottom of the canyon.

Sin created a massive chasm between man and God. One that none of us can cross. We are all guilty of some shortcoming. Society, by necessity, evaluates these shortcomings in degrees. Murder is punishable by death in some states. Theft will earn you prison time. Fraud may end in jail or hefty fines. Other things, like pride or hatred, may get you ostracized. Many are ignored. Some are celebrated. But when it comes to sin, a miss is a miss. Some may miss by miles, while others only miss by a few inches, but in our own power, we all end up at the bottom of the canyon. We all sin at some point, which puts us outside of God's glory.

Paul goes on to say that believers are *"justified as a gift by His grace through the redemption which is in Christ Jesus"* (v24). There's our ticket to a free ride across the sin chasm. Redemption is an exchange or transfer. We are destined to crash, but Christ exchanges His perfect sacrifice for all of our failures and gives us God's favor as a gift. Nobody else can do this. Good works won't do it. Incantations and ritual prayers won't do it. Only Christ can cover our sin. This "new covenant," as the New Testament is also called, is not between God and man; it is between Father and Son. Christ is our entry into God's glory.

Jesus Christ was *"displayed publicly as a propitiation in His blood through faith"* (v25). There's that word again: *propitiation*. Christ puts us back in favor with God when we put our faith in Him. That's the only requirement on our part: we must believe. In doing so, we acknowledge our own inability to obtain God's favor and earn our own salvation. A true believer admits that he or she is not good enough, while trusting that Christ's work is sufficient to cover all of his or her sins – the inches and the miles.

"This was to demonstrate His righteousness," Paul says, *"because in the forbearance of God He passed over the sins previously committed; for the demonstration, I say, of His righteousness at the present time, so that He would be just and the justifier of the one who has faith in Jesus"* (v25–26). We don't trust in our own righteousness because we have none. Instead, we put our faith in Jesus. His righteousness stands before God and says that we are His. The one requirement is at the end of that last verse: *"the one who has faith in Jesus."* Faith is "belief with the predominate idea of trust" and "a strong and welcome conviction."[2] It's the thinking upon which we build our lives, confident that it is true.

Jesus Christ vouches for His friends. He paid the price we cannot pay. His grace buys us a free ride across the canyon of sin. We must simply accept it and get to know Him personally. You take that worthless ticket with your name on it and exchange it for a ticket with His name printed on it, then get on board. You just need to claim that ticket through faith in Christ.

Get On Board

It is possible to buy a plane ticket, go to the airport, and sit in the terminal for the rest of your life. Churches are filled with people who have apparently decided this is as good as it gets. They accept the grace of Jesus, but never do anything with it. If you built the First Church of the Terminal, it would be filled with

....
[2] *Thayer and Smith. "Greek Lexicon entry for Pistis." "The NAS New Testament Greek Lexicon." 1999.*

people enjoying the food, fellowship, and nice view. We would put in a coffee shop, bring in a band, and spend an hour each week celebrating the fact that we have a boarding pass. Then we'd go home and do other things.

But if all there is to our Christian life is walking around the terminal and hanging out with other potential passengers, we never get beyond the gate. The truth is that if we're ever going to go anywhere, we have to get on board.

Have you ever noticed that you board an airplane one at a time? Nobody boards for you. You may line up in groups, but you go one-by-one through the checkpoint. We can congregate in groups in the terminal, but when it comes time to fly, every individual must make the decision to get on board. The same is true with our faith. We can go to church and be part of a group, but our faith can't really soar until we make that individual decision to fully get on board. Nobody can do it for you. You must purposely take the steps to engage in flight. Our intended journey will never begin as long as we stay comfortably on the ground. We can't even put one foot on the plane and pretend we're flying. We must get our ticket stamped (or scanned these days) and take our assigned seat.

When I board an airplane, I give up that thing I covet the most: control. As much as I'd prefer it, I don't go to the cockpit and allow the captain to be my co-pilot. I admit that I can't fly the aircraft, I take my seat, and rely on the crew to get us off the ground. It's a wholesale act of surrender, which can be a little frightening.

Andrew Murray wrote a great book on the subject called *Absolute Surrender*. He said, "We find the Christian life so difficult because we seek for God's blessing while we live in our own will." Getting on board means we surrender to someone else's control.

Our fate is no longer determined by our own will or actions, but relies completely on another.

The disciples exhibited this type of surrender as they followed Christ. One such instance occurred when Lazarus died. Jesus had just informed the disciples that He was going back to Judea, which concerned them because the Jewish leaders there were trying to kill Him. They had just left the area and retreated to the countryside because of the danger.

"Rabbi," the disciples said, "the Jews were just now seeking to stone You, and are You going there again?" This is the classic human response. We ask Jesus, "Are You sure? Is that really what You want?" We commit to follow Him, then hesitate when He calls us to go somewhere we're not sure about. We can easily be like the rich young ruler who told Jesus that he had followed the law, then asked what he was still lacking. Jesus gave him a simple instruction, but the man walked away. He was able to live up to the rules, but complete obedience was too much for him to handle. He wanted to maintain control.

When Jesus assured His disciples that He wanted to return to Judea, He explained why. "Our friend Lazarus has fallen asleep; but I go, so that I may awaken him out of sleep."

"Lord, if he has fallen asleep, he will recover," His disciples responded. Jesus was, of course, using a euphemism to describe Lazarus' death, so He put it plainly.

"Lazarus is dead," He said, then added, "and I am glad for your sakes that I was not there, so that you may believe; but let us go to him."

This was a decision point for those twelve. They didn't understand why Jesus was doing what He was doing. They were unsure about where He was going. To their reasoning, it was not the smart thing to do. But Thomas stepped up with the ultimate surrender. *"Let us also go,"* he said to the others, *"so that we may die with Him."* [3]

That's not just commitment, that's total abandonment. He could have said, "Let's go to protect Jesus," or, "Maybe we can sneak in unnoticed." But he was convinced they were marching to their deaths. Still, he was willing to go. Surrender is commitment to the point of death. It's going forward even when it makes no sense. For most of us, we don't face the threat of death, yet the principle is the same.

Jesus said, *"If anyone wishes to come after Me, he must deny himself, and take up his cross daily and follow Me"* (Luke 9:23). When we truly get on board, we deny ourselves by ceding control to Christ. There's no such thing as halfway surrender. We either maintain control or we let it go.

This is the issue we face on a daily basis. Will we settle for knowing that we have that ticket to Heaven while living our lives as we see fit, or will we go all-in and allow Christ to lead us to new places? It won't always make sense because we don't have the full cockpit view. We can barely see past today. We don't know where our words or actions will ultimately take us, and it's a little scary to surrender control to the unknown. Yet this is where a living, exciting faith starts.

Jesus warned, *"For whoever wishes to save his life will lose it; but whoever loses his life for My sake will find it"* (Matthew 16:25). What we often forget is that by maintaining control of our lives, we fail to discover the life Christ has planned for us. But staying comfortably on the ground means going nowhere. Holding on

....
[3] *John 11:7–16*

means missing out. We must move beyond commitment and totally surrender.

The good news is that when we lose our lives for His sake, we find life. Obviously this is a figure of speech, because Jesus doesn't lead us all to our physical death. Like the disciples who followed Him to Judea, we gain the privilege of seeing Christ work in miraculous ways. If they held back, they would not have seen Lazarus come out of the grave. They would have missed out on arguably the greatest miracle Christ performed. By submitting their will to His, they witnessed the power of Christ in an astonishing way.

This is the invitation He makes to us. Surrender your mediocre life and discover something more amazing, more powerful, and more life-changing than you could ever imagine. But to do so, you must get on board completely.

Stay On Board

I like to book a seat on the emergency row, preferably on the wing. They always ask if I'm willing and capable to open the door if needed and I always tell them, "If there's an emergency, you won't have to ask. I'll get the door open!"

But what if I decided to leave the plane in mid-flight? I'm not sure if those doors will even open at 30,000 feet, and I don't particularly want to find out. It would definitely be a disaster for me and many others. I would certainly be in worse shape than if I'd never boarded the flight, but the potential fallout for those also on board would pose a significant threat as well.

That's often what it's like when people "get on board" with Jesus Christ and then walk away. By this I'm not talking about simply committing a sin. Salvation isn't perfection, but it should be a process of being perfected. Even so, when you stumble down the aisle of an airplane, you're still moving in the right direction.

I've been on flights where unexpected turbulence catches people off guard, even throwing those standing into the laps of others. I've had to grab the backs of seats to stay upright. While it's not fun, it's usually not disastrous. Those who lose their balance simply make their way back to safety as they continue on their journey. But if someone decided to bail out of the plane during the flight, their odds of recovering would be slim to none.

This is how serious it is for those who truly walk with Christ and then walk away. We've all seen it. I could list names you'd probably recognize of those who have turned from Christ to embrace all manner of sin. A pastor friend of mine now sanctions homosexuality and other sin in his church. I've seen a pastor leave his family for another woman and watched the fallout. A former chaplain of mine now claims to be an atheist. It's painful. Innocent people get hurt. Loved ones are left bewildered, shocked, and devastated. Former members of their churches become disillusioned, pessimistic, or misled themselves.

That's why Jesus told someone who expressed a desire to follow Him after tending to his affairs, *"No one, after putting his hand to the plow and looking back, is fit for the kingdom of God"* (Luke 9:62). He wasn't trying to be a hard case or put the man off. He was warning against the perils of getting on board and not staying on board. He used a farming analogy, but the airplane analogy speaks the same truth. It's for our own good that once we begin to follow Him, we stick with it. He intends to take us to greater heights, but that also means it's a long way back down to where we began. It's not merely insulting to Him, but catastrophic for us.

Judas Iscariot did just that. He was more than a follower of Christ; he was one of the chosen twelve. If anyone was on board, it should have been him. But he didn't buy into Jesus' plan. He devised his own and pursued it to his own demise. I can only imagine that the other eleven were hurt as well. Judas was one of their own – a brother. It would have made sense for Christ to be betrayed by someone outside of their close circle, but from *within*? It had to be devastating. Most of all, it ruined Judas. He despaired to the point of suicide. His name went down in history as a traitor. All because he followed Jesus Christ, then went his own way.

The entire Old Testament records the Israelites' on-again, off-again relationship with God. After their dramatic deliverance from Egyptian slavery, God was visibly *"going before them in a pillar of cloud by day to lead them on the way, and in a pillar of fire by night to give them light"* (Exodus 13:22). After many years of brutal enslavement, they were free. All they had to do was look to the sky to see that God was leading their way. Yet even before they reached the Red Sea, some were ready to bail. As the Egyptian army pursued them, some said *"it would have been better for us to serve the Egyptians than to die in the wilderness"* (Exodus 14:12).

Moses replied, *"Do not fear! Stand by and see the salvation of the Lord . . . [who] will fight for you while you keep silent"* (Exodus 14:13–14). He was basically telling them, *"Sit down, buckle up, and keep quiet!"* This was the advice of the Psalmist when he said, *"Be still, and know that I am God"* (Psalm 46:10, NIV). Another translation says, *"Cease striving and know that I am God."* The connotation is to let go and relax because God is in control.

When we feel like bailing out, we must remember that we are not in control. Instead of fearing this truth, we must rest in it. Relax. Let go. God will take us where we need to go. Second-guessing or fretting over it only causes us problems. When we trust in Him instead of our own rationale and admit that His ways are superior to our own, He will put us on that higher trajectory.[4]

After the Israelites witnessed the supernatural parting of the Red Sea and the destruction of their enemy, they responded the right way – praise.

> *"The Lord is my strength and song, and He has become my salvation; This is my God, and I will praise Him . . . "*
>
> Exodus 15:2

Trust and praise is the solution when we're feeling doubt and anxiety. And really, it's not so much to convince God as it is to reassure ourselves. He knows our hearts. He knows how fickle humanity can be. He is incredibly patient, gracious, and merciful. We just need to stay on board with Him.

Shortly after their miraculous rescue and the destruction of the Egyptian army, God began providing the Israelites with bread and meat in the form of manna and quail. At God's instruction, Moses told the people to gather enough for one day. Of course, they didn't listen. But when they measured what people gathered, *"he who had gathered much had no excess, and he who had gathered little had no lack"* (Exodus 16:18). Moses told them not to keep it overnight, but of course some did. Consequently, they found it foul and full of worms. God asked, *"How long do you refuse to keep My commandments and My instructions?"* (Exodus 16:28).

Thousands of years later, we are much the same. We get on board with God's plan and then question Him. We want to pop

---

[4] *Proverbs 3:5*

the emergency exit in mid-air. God provides for us each day, but we want to hoard His blessings from the past so we don't have to depend on Him daily. We want to maintain some semblance of control. But that idea always rots. We were not created to be self-sufficient or dependent on any man. We were made to rely on Him and Him alone.

Something in our human nature (that would be sin) causes us to react negatively to this arrangement. But imagine a man who questioned the flight attendant about the emergency door at 30,000 feet. "Why the rules? Who put you in charge? I'm in control of my own destiny; I'll open that door and go my own way any time I please!"

First of all, the flight attendant would think the man was insane. He or she would try to explain the danger his thinking posed, not just to the other passengers but primarily to himself. When the bullheaded passenger still refused to listen, the attendant might try to restrain him. If that failed, he or she might call for help. If the man persisted to the point of reaching the door, there would come a point when others would run for their own lives. The man would quickly discover the vicious fall awaiting him on the other side of his foolishness. If conscious, he might even curse the others still on the airplane for abandoning him.

If you've been in the church very long, you've seen this type of behavior. Like some of the Israelites, people repeatedly ignore God's instructions. They complain about "rules" when it's really God's gracious revelation of life-giving truth. They spurn those who would help them and try to go their own way. Then the door blows open and they get sucked out by their own foolish ways. They may even blame those still on board with God's plan. But in the end, they hit the ground. Every time. Some falls take longer than others, but the ground is always there, unforgiving and inflexible.

It may be possible to crawl back to the terminal and board another flight, but what a painful process! It's far easier to listen to the instructions of God and stick with them. If you stumble, stay in the aisle. You can get up. To plow that straight, effective line, you must keep your eyes forward. To find your way through the wilderness, you simply need to look up. And to get to that wonderful destination, you simply need to buckle up and stay on board.

Chapter 2

THE PASSPORT

Anyone who travels overseas knows that the one thing you keep secured at all times is your passport. It's the little booklet that holds vital information about who you are and authorizes you to go places. Without it, going anywhere is very difficult, if not impossible. As believers, we need something to show who we are and empower us to go places. The Word of God serves as our passport. It affirms our identity in Christ and authorizes us to fulfill His mission. We carry it in our hearts. It was written before we ever showed up for the flight, but we need it wherever we go. Without it, going anywhere is very difficult, if not impossible.

Your Name

The most significant information on a passport is your name. It confirms who you are to the world and even to yourself. Without it, it's easy to go through life with a spiritual Jason Bourne syndrome. If you haven't seen the movies, he's the Robert Ludlum character who suffers from lack of oxygen to the brain and spends several movies trying to figure out who he is. It makes for an interesting plot, but a miserable life. Along the way, Bourne finds multiple passports with his photo on them, which gets him in and out of places, but doesn't truly confirm his identity. The fictional character is constantly mired in confusion, doesn't know who to trust, and wastes a lot of time trying to figure out what the heck is going on!

When we become followers of Christ, we take up His name as "Christians." Looking to His Word to find out what that means enables us to follow the plot line of God's plan. If we look to multiple sources for our identity, it's terribly confusing. When we discover that God's Word contains our one true identity, we can be at peace in our own mind and boldly proclaim who we are to the rest of the world.

As you embark on your God-given journey, you need your passport with your God-given name written in it. It proves who you are. It's the only set of credentials you need in life. If the world doubts you or your head gets mixed up (like Jason Bourne), just look at your spiritual passport. It holds your true identity and gives you access into new places.

So who are you? You might be surprised to hear that "Christian" is a slave term. At least that's how Paul saw it. *"This letter is from Paul,"* he begins his message to the Romans, *"a slave of Christ Jesus . . . "* (NLT). Most translations shy away from the term "slave" in favor of "servant" or "bond-servant," but the Greek word is *duolos*, which expressly means "slave."

Murray Harris, author of the book *Slave of Christ*, relates the sentiment of Dr. Josef Tson, a Romanian pastor arrested, imprisoned, and exiled for his faith. "A servant gives service to someone, but a slave belongs to someone. We commit ourselves to do something, but when we surrender ourselves to someone, we give ourselves up."

The distinction is significant. Servants are hired; slaves are owned. This is the term used repeatedly in Scripture, and it's precisely the imagery the apostle intended. But Paul wasn't alone. Mary, the mother of Jesus, used it (in the feminine) when she responded to the angel Gabriel: *"And Mary said, 'Behold, the doule of the Lord; may it be done to me according to your word'"* (Luke 1:38). James, Peter, and Jude introduced themselves as *duolos* in their letters[1]. Luke used the term in Acts: *"Lord . . . grant that Your duolos may speak Your word with all confidence"* (Acts 4:29). John used it in Revelation: *"And a voice came from the throne, saying, 'Give praise to our God, all you His duolos, you who fear Him, the small and the great"* (Revelation 19:5). And Jesus used it to communicate His disciples' relationship to Him: *"Remember the word that I said to you, 'A duolos is not greater than his master.' If they persecuted Me, they will also persecute you; if they kept My word, they will keep yours also"* (John 15:20).

The term is purposeful and inescapable. As John MacArthur points out in his book entitled *Slave*, "The Gospel is not simply an invitation to become Christ's associate; it is a mandate to become His slave."

As slaves, we are bought with a price[2], forsake all others[3], serve only one master[4], and strive only to please Him[5]. Once we understand this paradigm shift, we can begin to properly understand

....

[1] *James 1:1, 2 Peter 1:1, Jude 1*
[2] *1 Corinthians 6:20*
[3] *Luke 14:33*
[4] *Matthew 6:24*
[5] *2 Corinthians 5:9*

much more of the Scriptural role to which we are called. Despite the bumper sticker, God is not simply our "co-pilot" flying along-side us through life. He is our Lord and Master to whom we give account for our actions; our flight instructor, calling the shots and instructing us to a successful flight.

Slavery is complete submission to the Master. Just as earthly slaves take on the identity of their owner (often marked or branded with his name), depend on the master for every provision, and act only under the instruction and on behalf of the master, we, as spiritual slaves, must do the same. This is not a passive position. To the contrary, as a slave we are to act on our Master's behalf, working, investing what He has trusted to us, and multiplying His investment in us. Otherwise, we are likened to the "wicked" slave who merely held[6] what he was given and did nothing with it. When we truly give ourselves wholly to Him, we voluntarily forfeit the right to live life for ourselves.

"You are not your own," Paul declares in 1 Corinthians 6. This grates heavily on the modern, western mindset. We value our independence and self-sufficiency. We implore the Master to act on our behalf. We set our own goals and attempt to use God to achieve them. This is completely backwards. We cannot rightly say that Jesus is Lord if we do not realize that we are His slaves.

The idea of slavery has a diabolical connotation for most of us, and rightly so. Slavery to anything but God is evil and in some cases idolatrous. According to Jesus, *"Everyone who commits sin is the slave of sin"* (John 8:34). One may wonder why God has allowed so much slavery to inflict suffering on the human race. It is, no doubt, a part of the fallen nature of man. But perhaps it's

....
[6] *Matthew 25:26*

also to demonstrate the consequences of selling out to anything except Christ.

Bob Dylan had it right when he wrote in a song, "It may be the devil or it may be the Lord, but you're gonna have to serve somebody." Paul said, *"Do you not know that when you present yourselves to someone as slaves for obedience, you are slaves of the one whom you obey, either of sin resulting in death, or of obedience resulting in righteousness?"* (Romans 6:16). From the apostles to modern songwriters, this idea of subservience to someone or something rings true because it is the very nature of mankind to submit. No matter how hard we fight it, we all submit in the end – to time, entropy, and eventually death. The good news is that we serve a Master who is not only good, but the very definition of goodness. Our Master promises to provide our every need,[7] never leave or forsake us[8], and prepare a glorious home for us.[9] And through His unmatched grace, He takes our willingness to submit to Him a step further: He adopts us as sons and daughters!

The practice of slave adoption was not common in the first century, but it was not foreign. In both the Old and New Testament times, a master could adopt a slave. But doing so came with a price. You see, a son or daughter could be disowned by a father. A slave could be sold or even killed. But an adopted slave remained a child of the father forever. There was no going back in this matter. It was and still is a permanent status, and one that God extends to us when we willingly become His slave.

....

[7] *Philippians 4:19*

[8] *Matthew 28:20, Hebrews 13:5*

[9] *John 14:2, 3*

"In love He predestined us to adoption as sons through Jesus Christ to Himself, according to the kind intention of His will, to the praise of the glory of His grace, which He freely bestowed on us in the Beloved."

Ephesians 1:4b–6

Slavery is a condition we must first enter into in order to be eligible for adoption. God does not adopt strangers, nor does He adopt part-time servants. He only adopts those whom He has purchased.

"But when the fullness of the time came, God sent forth His Son, born of a woman, born under the Law, so that He might redeem *those who were under the Law, that we might receive the adoption as sons."*

Galatians 4:4–5 (emphasis added)

The word "redeem" here is *exagorazo* in Greek, which means "by payment of a price to recover from the power of another, to ransom, buy off." Sin once owned you, like a slave is owned. But Christ paid that debt on the cross. Paul used the same language in Romans 3:24 when he said that believers are *"justified as a gift by His grace through the redemption which is in Christ Jesus."* Here "redemption" is in the noun form – *apolutrosis* in Greek. It means "liberation procured by the payment of a ransom." Christ recovered you from sin's power. The law demanded a price (death) and Jesus paid it, so the law has been bought off. The ransom is fulfilled and you are now owned by Christ and elevated to an adopted child eternally joined with the Father.

This is God's plan for each of us. Jesus Christ conquered sin and paid the price for us, so we must not continue to be slaves to sin. *"The slave [to sin] does not remain in the house forever; the son does remain forever"* (John 8:35).

Jesus warned that we will face trials and James promised that our faith will be tested, but that's not the same as being a slave to sin. Unlike slaves, we fight sin with the promise of winning the war. When we forsake all other masters and intentionally sell out to Christ, our relationship to sin is no longer as a slave, but as a warrior triumphantly fighting against it.

Paul also says, *"The Spirit Himself testifies with our spirit that we are children of God, and if children, heirs also, heirs of God and fellow heirs with Christ, if indeed we suffer with Him so that we may also be glorified with Him"* (Romans 8:14–17).

Think about that: Your heavenly Father owns everything. He created the universe. And you are in a position to inherit it! When that sinks in, it makes it hard to worry about much. No matter what you go through, you know what happens in the end – you get more than you can imagine! All believers are on a Heaven-bound ride, so no matter how rough the flight may be, the destination is glorious.

For now, however, you are an ambassador for Christ. That means you represent Christ here on earth. You operate under His authority and live under His covering. Your home is an embassy – property belonging to the kingdom of Heaven – and your King provides whatever you need to fulfill your mission.

You are also part of a chosen generation, a royal priesthood, and a holy nation.[10] There is no better passport than one with those credentials! It says *"citizen of heaven"* (Philippians 3:20).

....
[10] *1 Peter 2:9*

You are the light in a dark world.[11] God is no longer your enemy; He is your friend.[12] You are not destined for destruction, because you are an overcomer[13] and more than a conqueror.[14] You are not damaged goods, you are healed.[15] You are not deficient, you are complete.[16]

This is how God sees you; therefore, this is how you must see yourself. You must believe the name printed on your spiritual passport. This is part of being a believer – you believe what God says about you. If you don't truly believe that this identity is actually *you*, you won't be able to fulfill the mission He has in store. You must believe Him when He tells you who you are.

Your Passport Number

All passports are simultaneously the same and unique. Every one is a little booklet that declares pretty much the same basic information about a person. Yet no two are alike because they testify to the uniqueness of every human being. We use unique numbers to ensure that "John Smith" from Oregon is not the same as "John Smith" from Virginia. Despite potential similarities in hair color, eye color, height, origin, and other external factors, each person is different because we are all individuals.

Since I was adopted, I grew up seeing similarities between my sisters and my parents that I never had. This was never a negative thing; I knew the meaning of "family," so there was no disappointment or alienation or anything else. It was just a fact. That's why

[11] Matthew 5:14
[12] John 15:15
[13] Revelation 12:11
[14] Romans 8:37
[15] 1 Peter 2:24
[16] Colossians 2:10

having children of my own was such a strange, frightening, and exhilarating experience. For the first time, I knew someone who was my flesh and blood relation.

With the first two children, my wife and I sort of cloned ourselves. My daughter has my wife's red hair and many of her personality traits. My son favors me heavily, both in appearance and personality. Then we switched it up. My younger son favors my wife's side of the family a little more, though the resemblance isn't quite as clear. My youngest daughter definitely leans my direction. It's really weird. We couldn't have planned it this way if we had tried. At times we see ourselves in them, through physical expressions, as well as less tangible things like music choices, food preferences, hobbies, and mannerisms.

At the same time, some really unique things have popped up over the years. My oldest daughter is studying art on a college scholarship and gets paid to do oil paintings. No art done by my wife or me is worthy of even hanging in the garage! My oldest son enjoys fishing, which ranks around knitting in my list of hobbies. When forced (by me) to get involved in school sports, my younger son spurned football and baseball (my sports) and chose lacrosse (I didn't even know it existed in Texas). My youngest daughter is so much of an independent spirit that listing her unique traits would take too long. I would have never predicted these things. Even though I feel like I know them better than anyone else on earth, each individual child of mine is so complex and different that there could never be a substitute for any one of them. We are all family – that much is obvious – yet we are all unique.

Paul explained this simultaneous similarity and uniqueness by saying, *"we, who are many, are one body in Christ, and individually members one of another"* (Romans 1:5). It's imperative to understand the strength of our commonality in Christ as well as the significance of our individuality. Imbalance can result in either feeling irrelevant and unimportant on one end to self-centered and arrogant on the other. If we think we're lost in the mass of humanity, we deny the highly personal relationship God wants with each of us. But if we begin to think we're better than others, then in our minds, we cheapen God's love for them. The reality is that God's eternal plans continue with or without you. He doesn't need you, but He desires you. He invites you to partake in His kingdom now, here on earth. He gives you the power to experience it, promises to help you every step of the way, and wants to bless you by working through you. That's why He uniquely created you and enables you to interact with others in a way that only you can.

Jesus summed up the entire Old Testament law with two commandments: First, love God with all your heart, mind, and soul. This vertical paradigm is like the uniformity of passports. There is little room for variation. It's about as straightforward as it gets. We don't pay Jesus Christ lip service on Easter and Christmas. We don't merely show God respect for an hour on Sunday. And we don't think we love God while our heart pursues other things with more passion. We love God with *all*. That means there is nothing left over for things that are not of God. In that, all followers of Christ should be the same. Jesus demands *all* of us *all* the time, not part of us some of the time.

The second commandment is this: Love your neighbor as yourself. That's a simple, clear command, but how you carry that out is as unique as you are. Like the numbers in our passports, horizontal relationships are never the same between any two people. You relate to your spouse like nobody else on earth. The same is true for your children, your parents, your siblings, your boss, your co-workers, and everyone else in your life. Carrying out this edict looks different for everyone, giving you one-of-a-kind significance in God's plan.

Nobody can fulfill their role in God's great plan in the same way that you can. Nobody can go on your journey for you. He has placed a unique number in your spiritual passport. This inherent uniqueness makes you integral in His kingdom. It puts you in a position that nobody else can fill, giving you irreplaceable value. We are all of one body in Christ, but every part of the body is important.

Validation

A passport is only good if it's legitimate. Fakes exist and might appear convincing, but if tested it will be found to be fraudulent. To signify a passport's authenticity, governments stamp it with a seal. It shows citizenship and confirms one's right-standing. Spiritually, we need this stamp of approval, too, and there is only one thing that validates us in the eyes of God: the name of Jesus Christ. Every person that bears His name can enter into His presence; all others cannot.

The New Testament introduced a strange new idea: belief not merely in God, but in Jesus Christ. For centuries, the Israelites had proclaimed *Yahweh*, also known as the God of Jacob, the God of Abraham, and other similar titles. Then suddenly John the Baptist came on the scene, and he wasn't only pointing to a God in Heaven, but to a man on earth. He equated belief in God with belief in Jesus of Nazareth. This was radical and, if untrue, heretical.

When two of Christ's disciples, Peter and John, the son of Zebedee, were arrested in Jerusalem and brought before the high priest and other Jewish leaders, Peter pointed to *"Jesus Christ the*

Nazarene, whom you crucified, whom God raised from the dead," and proclaimed, *"there is salvation in no one else; for there is no other name under heaven that has been given among men by which we must be saved"* (Acts 4:10, 12).

This is one of several passages that use the phrase "the name" when referring to Jesus Christ. In the first chapter of John's Gospel, he begins by introducing John the Baptist (not the author), who came to announce the fulfillment of the Old Covenant with the arrival of the Messiah, Jesus Christ.

> *"But as many as received Him, to them He gave the right to become children of God, even to those who believe in His name, who were born, not of blood nor of the will of the flesh nor of the will of man, but of God."*
>
> John 1:12–13

He's talking about the Jewish people here, saying that they are not considered sons of God through natural birth, but that everyone who receives Christ is a child of God through spiritual birth – those who received Christ while He lived and those who "believe in His name." The verb translated as "receive" has the connotation "to associate with one's self as a companion." What a beautiful picture: When we take Jesus Christ as a companion, someone to walk alongside through life, we become a child of God. We are validated as His belonging.

I often hear people say, "We are all God's children." Not so. Jesus said to the Jewish leaders of His day, *"If God were your Father, you would love Me . . . You are of your father the devil . . . "* (John 8:42–44). If the descendants of the chosen nation of Israel can no longer call themselves children of God, how can non-Jews even pretend to have any relationship with God the Father? It's only when we receive and recognize the divinity of Jesus Christ, acknowledge the work He did through His life, death, and resurrection, and believe in the truth He proclaimed can we be called a child of God.

The term "name" does not simply mean that by which one is called. The Greek *onoma* also signifies rank, authority, and deeds. It's not enough to pay lip service to a historic figure; we must recognize and acknowledge the position, power, and work of Jesus Christ. Those who say they believe in Jesus Christ, but ignore His rank, authority, and deeds expose their unbelief by their actions. According to His Word, He is the only begotten Son of God. He is the only way to gain entrance into Heaven. All truth resides in Him. He commands the angels, and demons must obey Him. If we believe in His name, we accept His authority in all matters. Otherwise, we do not believe.

The apostle John reiterates the power of His name when he discusses the purpose of his writing, saying, *"These have been written so that you may believe that Jesus is the Christ, the Son of God; and that believing you may have life in His name"* (John 20:31).

Paul invokes this idea repeatedly throughout his letters to the churches. When talking about salvation, he says that we were once sinners: *". . . but you were washed, but you were sanctified, but you were justified in the name of the Lord Jesus Christ and in the Spirit of our God"* (1 Corinthians 6:11). It is this recognition of the truth of Christ's authority and the accomplishment of His actions that allows us to receive eternal life even though we have not seen Him in person.

Validation only comes through Jesus Christ. It's not the generic name of "God" or the admission of a "higher power." Our sins are not justified through spiritualism, other religions, or church participation. Validation is only through one name – Jesus Christ.

My passport stamp of the United States of America signifies that I am a citizen of that country. It proclaims that I belong to America. Even if other countries reject me, I can always come home. The name of Jesus Christ stamped on your life means that you belong to Him. You have a home. As a citizen of God's Kingdom, you will increasingly become aware that this life is a journey; that you are wandering in a foreign land for a short time.

The funny thing about tourists is that they are easy to spot. I've been in the middle of nowhere in southern Africa and a local has walked up to me, taken one look at me, and said, "American!" Sometimes it's easy for others to figure it out by the clothes we wear, the music we listen to, and the books or newspapers we read. But even if we faked these things, our passport stamp would tell the truth.

Christians shouldn't be too hard to spot. While Paul does urge us to dress modestly, it should go deeper. *"Your adornment must not be merely external – braiding the hair, and wearing gold jewelry, or putting on dresses; but let it be the hidden person of the heart, with the imperishable quality of a gentle and quiet spirit, which is precious in the sight of God"* (1 Peter 3:3–4).

Americans especially focus on clothing and grooming, but do we spend as much time trying to be good (as in "Godly") as we do trying to look good? Do the things we listen to, read, and watch reinforce God's truth or do they work against it? Just as our clothes, hobbies, and other activities don't make us citizens of any country, the external things don't make us believers. Yet the internal things should be apparent on the outside.

Often the dead giveaway of our nationality lies in our accent. In the States, we realize there is a big difference between Boston and Austin, but to the rest of the world, we all sound like Americans.

Within the church, we may use different phrases to express our faith, but it will always impact our speech. By that, I don't mean that we will use "Christianese" catchphrases. Paul urges us "*. . . in speech, conduct, love, faith and purity, show yourself an example of those who believe*" (1 Timothy 4:12). Jesus said that our mouths peak from that which fills our hearts.[17] So it stands to reason that our very words will be accented with His love when we are filled with Him, and the world will hear it.

Another interesting thing about being an American when travelling abroad is that there are reminders everywhere of home. I've eaten a burger from Wendy's in Frankfort, watched ESPN in Johannesburg, and read a copy of USA *Today* in a Hong Kong hotel room and felt like I was almost home. God not only gives us reminders of our spiritual home, but He brings it to us wherever we are. Jesus continually proclaimed, *"The kingdom of heaven is at hand."*[18] When He ascended into Heaven, He promised that He would always be with us.[19]

To me, it's a bit like when the NFL or NHL plays a game in London or Stockholm. For Americans who are overseas, those games are a taste of the U.S. right where they are. Living with the Holy Spirit is a taste of perfect Heaven right here in this fallen world. It's a reminder that even though we are *in* this world, we are not *of* this world. Our names are sealed in God's book, waiting for the day that we join Him for eternity. In the meantime, we travel this life "in the name of Jesus" with His likeness imprinted on our lives, validating us as His children and empowering us to walk in His authority.

....

[17] *Luke 6:45*

[18] *Matthew 3:2, 4:17, 10:7, Mark 1:15*

[19] *Matthew 28:20*

Chapter 3

TAKING OFF

A journey that never leaves the ground is not a journey at all. Mountains and oceans create natural barriers that can't be overcome without some help. Spiritually, this world has too many natural barriers that prevent us from going far on our own. We must rise above the things of this world to really take off.

Lift

In order for an airplane to leave the ground, it has to create what's known in aeronautics as *lift*. Technically, an airplane could work as a really big, really fast bus. One could taxi from Chicago to St. Louis faster than one could drive, but that would be pretty dumb. The mass of freeway required and the cost of jet fuel would render it pointless. A high-speed train makes more sense.

Yet many Christians think that by being really busy with their religious activities, they are reaching new heights in their spiritual lives. Never mind the damage caused by their enormous wingspan or the traffic disruptions in their wake, they are flying – or so they imagine. In reality, faith that never gets off the ground fails to fulfill its purpose, no matter how noisy it sounds or impressive it looks. Without *lift*, an airplane is just an expensive disruption.

So how does an airplane create *lift*? The simple answer is that it changes the air to create the right kind of force. For jets, the wings force an incredible amount of air downward in order to lift it upward. But for the purpose of the analogy, I want to focus on two things: change and force.

Change comes through belief in Jesus Christ. We all have faith in something. Passengers have faith in the pilots. Secular scientists have faith in their ever-changing theories. Christians have faith in Jesus Christ.

Interestingly, the word "belief" does not appear in the New American Standard translation of the Bible. It appears only once in the King James Version and that reference is translated "faith" in other versions. The English world "faith" appears in the Greek as *pistis*. Note the similarity to the Greek word for "believe," which is *pistueo*. They are the noun and verb, respectively, of the same idea. Faith is the thing one holds to be true. Believing puts it into practice. It's something you have to actually do, not just think about doing. It is being persuaded that something is true, putting your confidence in it, and trusting to the point of rock-solid conviction. Real faith always translates into action.

If you won the lottery, you might buy a house or a car. You might go on an exotic vacation. You'd act on it. But if you didn't believe you actually had the money, you wouldn't attempt to spend thousands of dollars (or at least you shouldn't!). Put it this way: If you were trying to buy a house and the bank didn't believe you'd won the lottery, you wouldn't get the house, no matter how much you protested.

Jesus said, *"'The kingdom of heaven is like a treasure hidden in the field, which a man found and hid again; and from joy over it he goes and sells all that he has and buys that field'"* (Matthew 13:44). When we truly find that piece of Heaven in our lives, we gladly give up everything that prevents us from fully owning it. We lay down our short-sighted ambitions to participate in the more exciting life God has in store. We hurry to cast down the dead idols that stand in the way of a relationship with the living God. Once we understand the value of that "buried treasure," there is nothing worth holding onto when compared to kingdom life in Christ.

The point is that belief is something that you base your entire life upon. Your thoughts change. Your behaviors change. You are a completely different person – a new person, in fact. A starving man who receives food eats it. And really, belief in Jesus Christ is like dining on a spiritual feast, because you discover that all of your legitimate cravings are satisfied. Your table overflows with love, joy, peace, patience, kindness, goodness, faithfulness, gentleness, and self-control. You have to partake of it to receive its nourishment, but it's yours. And when you believe it, you act like it.

John the Baptist preceded Jesus Christ's ministry on earth by declaring, *"'The time is fulfilled, and the kingdom of God is at hand; repent and believe in the gospel'"* (Mark 1:15). The gospel is the good news that Jesus Christ, the promised Messiah, has arrived. Believe it. Act like it.

John 3:16 is the gospel on a poster because it simply states *". . . whoever believes in Him [Jesus] shall not perish, but have eternal life."* Jesus said, *"Unless you believe that I am He [God], you will die in your sins."* As He said these things, it says a few verses later, many came to *believe* in Him.[1] Before Jesus raised His friend Lazarus from the dead, He said to Martha, who was grieving over his death, *"'I am the resurrection and the life; he who believes in Me will live even if he dies, and everyone who lives and believes in Me will never die.'"* He pushed her on the subject: *"'Do you believe this?'"* Her response was simple and direct. *"'Yes, Lord; I have believed that You are the Christ, the Son of God, even He who comes into the world'"* (John 11:25–27). This is salvation.

Later, after Christ was crucified, resurrected, and ascended into Heaven, His disciples preached this simple message. When Paul and Silas were freed from prison because of an earthquake, the jailer asked, "What must I do to be saved?" They didn't tell him to do any of the things people often suggest we do to save ourselves: atone for our sins, become like God, or some other human machination. He didn't join a denomination. He didn't give an offering or make a sacrifice. He didn't even bow his head and say a prayer. *"'Believe in the Lord Jesus, and you will be saved,'"* they said. The jailer did, and his salvation came immediately. He and his whole family were then baptized.[2]

Paul later wrote about salvation to the Romans, who didn't know the Jewish traditions or Old Testament, and said, *"... that if you confess with your mouth Jesus as Lord, and believe in your heart that God raised Him from the dead, you will be saved ..."* (Romans 10:9).

There's a definite pattern there! I think the reason people want to add to that is because it's very easy to just pay lip service to belief. But genuine belief changes everything about a person. It changes

....
[1] *John 8:24–30*
[2] *Acts 16:30–4*

the way they think about themselves and others. It changes the way they talk (and I don't mean the use of church clichés). It changes what they do and how they do it. The changed person can't hide it, and those around him or her can't deny it. It's like waking up. Before, you were lying there snoring or maybe mumbling incoherent things. You may have tossed and turned a bit. But now you're walking around doing things, carrying on conversations, and living life. Once you actually believe that Jesus Christ is truth, you awaken to an entirely new world – and it shows because everything changes.

Faith that changes nothing is worthless because it lacks the force to move anything within us or around us. When an airplane pushes air downward, it creates enough force to lift hundreds of tons. That's an amazing amount of force. So what can faith do? Jesus told His disciples, "'. . . *Truly I say to you, if you have faith and do not doubt . . . if you say to this mountain, "Be taken up and cast into the sea," it will happen. And all things you ask in prayer, believing, you will receive'*" (Matthew 21:21–22). I admit this is a passage that I don't fully understand, because people don't literally throw around mountains, and even the most faithful, earnest prayers don't always get answered in the way we want, but clearly Jesus was making a point about the power of faith. There is more force there than we realize.

We must personally experience that power to fully understand what He is communicating. I have seen some amazing answers to prayer. I've seen people survive impossible situations. I've witnessed completely hopeless people become entirely new creatures. Suffice to say that I've experienced enough force in my own life and in the lives of others to know that we've only scratched the surface of Christ's power.

Faith is the force that enables change. It holds the power to transform the atmosphere in and around us. It's impossible to summarize in a few words how faith can change your world, but when engaged, it gives you the lift necessary to soar to new heights.

Shape

The secret to obtaining and maintaining *lift*, which enables flight, lies in the shape of the wing. Engineers can't build exciting or creative designs for the sake of artistic style. They must fashion precise structures specifically calibrated to the demands of the aircraft. They modify their design when they discover a flaw because they are always working to maximize its ability in relation to the laws of physics. There are absolutes at work, so the shape of the wings must conform to those unchanging truths in order to succeed.

Faith is the same way. We cannot create our own belief system and pretend it's as good as anything else. We don't find "our own" truth. We must fashion our ideas specifically conditioned to the demands of God's truth. When we discover a flaw within ourselves, we correct it because we are always growing in knowledge. There are absolutes at work, so the shape of our faith must conform to those unchanging truths in order to succeed.

Many professing believers can't get any *lift* in their spiritual lives because their wings of belief are the wrong shape. It may be intentional or unintentional, but the result is the same when our lives don't line up with the truth of God. So how do we know what is true? Is it even possible?

Jesus' disciples struggled with this idea. They were trying to follow Christ, but even with Him right there, they found it difficult to fully understand truth. *"Thomas said to Him, 'Lord, we do not know where You are going, how do we know the way?' Jesus said to* him, 'I am they way, and the truth, and the life . . . ' Philip said to Him, 'Lord, show us the Father, and it is enough for us.' Jesus said to him . . . 'He who has seen Me has seen the Father . . . .'"[3]

We are guilty of asking the wrong question. We want to know, "What is truth?" We should be asking, "Who is truth?" The answer is Jesus Christ. He wasn't merely a good teacher or even a prophet for His time. He is the essence of truth. Paul says that we have *"put on the new self who is being renewed to a true knowledge according to the image of the One who created him"* (Colossians 3:10). The idea communicated in Greek is that as new creations in Christ, we are growing into a precise and correct knowledge in the likeness of God. Our minds are transformed so that we can know the truth that makes us look like Him. We change the shape of who we are so that it looks less like us and more like him.

When I was a kid, my dad would take me to the M.E. Moses Five & Dime, one of the last remaining stores of its type. This place was great. They sold all sorts of odd things, including balsa glider planes painted to look like WWII fighters. These were simple, lightweight constructions, but they could really fly! Four simple pieces of wood fit together to make an airplane about a foot long. I spent countless hours launching these things in and outdoors.

It wasn't until many years later I realized that *balsa* is a type of tree. If you had asked me what *balsa* was when I was younger, I'd have said an airplane. I realized it was wood, but it had been cut and painted into a shape that made it look more like a glider than a tree. It had been conformed to the image of a plane so that the "treeness" was hidden. This is a rudimentary glimpse of what

....
[3] John 14:5–6, 8–9

it looks like when we conform to the image of Christ. Our old shape, or belief system, changes as His truth is revealed.

Philosophers love to debate ideas of truth and whether we can rely on any of them. To me, it's a bit like debating the shape of an airplane's wing. When you're on the ground, you can talk all you want. But when you're in the air, it better fly. And the reality is that some shapes fly better than others.

Still, intellectually astute people like to debate. The radical skeptic doubts that any idea is better than another. The mitigated skeptic believes some things to be more reliable than others, but agrees that certainty is unattainable. These are the debates of those who have never flown.

Rene Descartes formulated two hypotheses of skepticism. According to the "Dream Hypothesis," we cannot know at any particular moment that we are not dreaming. Therefore, everything is subject to our own self-centered conjuring. The "Demon Hypothesis" postulates that an external, malevolent demon could make us believe with absolute certainty something that is absolutely false. Fortunately, Christ relieves us of self-reliant or demonic influences by assuring us that we can know truth by knowing Christ. We can attain a shape that we know for sure flies.

I had the privilege to interview Frank Turek, a brilliant writer and apologist. In his book *I Don't Have Enough Faith to Be an Atheist,* he and co-author Dr. Norman Geisler outline six characteristics of truth.

First, truth is discovered, not invented. It exists independently of anyone's knowledge of it. It's generally accepted in American history that the Wright brothers invented flight (claims by Félix du Temple de la Croix, Alexander Fyodorovich Mozhayskiy, Clément Ader, Sir Hiram Maxim, Augustus Moore Herring, Karl Jatho, Gus

Stamps, and Richard Pearse notwithstanding). But really, they just discovered it. Flight was always possible; mankind just hadn't possessed the knowledge to achieve it yet. Jesus Christ made truth even easier than the pursuit of flight. He revealed it when He was born over 2,000 years ago. We need not invent it; we simply need to discover it by acknowledging Him and allowing our minds to be renewed into His likeness.

Second, truth transcends culture and time. Absolute truth is the same for everyone, everywhere, at all times. Of course, some situations apply to some people that don't apply to others, like the fact that Christopher Columbus didn't have airplanes while we do, but the laws of physics were exactly the same then as they are now. Our understanding of them has changed over time, but they operated no differently in Noah's age, Nero's age, Newton's age, or now. That's why the truth of Christ is the same today, yesterday, and forever. In Him, there is no male or female, Jew or gentile, black or white, first-century believer or 21st century believer.[4] Obviously, as an American man of English-Irish descent in 2014, I am different than Empress Wu Zetian in China's seventh-century Tang Dynasty, but the truth of Jesus Christ applied precisely the same for her then as it does for me now.

Third, truth is unchanging even though our beliefs about truth change. My great-grandfather, born in 1878, probably thought flight was not possible when he was a boy. But by the time he died in 1966, he himself had flown. The reality of flight didn't change, merely his generation's understanding and implementation of it. In 2008, a tribe in the thick rainforest on the Brazilian-Peruvian border was photographed for the first time by a low-flying airplane.

....
4 *Galatians 3:28*

These uncontacted people, many painted red from head to toe, shot arrows at the plane, likely believing it to be a threatening bird or evil spirit, as was common among previously uncontacted tribes. But their ignorance has no bearing on the truth. It is the same with the truth of Jesus Christ. We can shoot all the arrows we want at Him and everything He stands for, but our ignorance doesn't change a thing. He is who He is, regardless of our errant beliefs.

Fourth, beliefs cannot change a fact, no matter how sincerely they are held. That tribe may have believed the flight that took the photograph was an evil spirit, but that didn't turn the photographer and pilot into demons. We can debate the existence of God, the veracity of Christ, or any number of things presented in the Bible. But that doesn't change the truth. Either He is the Messiah come to save the world or He wasn't. If, as Christians believe, He is who He says He is, then any other view has no bearing on the truth, no matter how earnestly people think otherwise.

Fifth, truth is not affected by the attitude of the one professing it. *"So will My word be which goes forth from My mouth,"* God said through the prophet Isaiah. *"It will not return to Me empty, without accomplishing what I desire, and without succeeding in the matter for which I sent it"* (Isaiah 55:11). Truth does what truth does with no regard for people. That's why even the most corrupt preacher can speak God's truth and people will come to Christ. Conversely, the nicest, most humble Taoist can pursue a path to enlightenment, but when he dies, he does not experience reincarnation because his noble ideas and firm convictions simply aren't true. In modern American culture, many people in the church are not aware of this truth, and it leads to unnecessary disappointment and disillusionment. I remember how shaken many people were when Jimmy Swaggart's admission of sin and subsequent revelations of prostitution hit the news. He had done so much to bring people into God's truth that when he failed, people couldn't separate the truth he declared from the man who declared it. But truth is truth even when our attitudes and actions don't line up with it. Our righteousness, or lack of it, doesn't change who Christ is.

Finally, absolute truths are always true. In physics, gravity pulls objects toward the earth, regardless of the object. It doesn't care if it's a feather or a Falcon 2,000 jet, gravity exerts its force on everything at all times. The absolute truths presented in the Bible are always true, regardless of who you are or what you've done. Jesus Christ is the answer for everyone. His forgiveness applies to your sins, no matter how bad they may be. His grace is sufficient not just for the housewife in Houston, but for the mafia hit man in Chicago. We cannot escape His love nor earn His favor. We can only acknowledge it and act on it. But understanding Him as truth doesn't change Him, it changes us.

When we conform to His truth and renew our minds daily through the power of the Holy Spirit, we shape our belief according to God's eternal laws, and He promises to lift us to new heights. This is the basis to a more fulfilling and impactful life. It's not some great secret or impossible puzzle. It's simply Jesus Christ. He is truth. He is the way to God. And He is the life that each of us needs.

Bent

So what kind of shape works best for flight? If you look at some old airplanes, you will see that the wings were pretty flat. That kind of shape could get you somewhere, but like the Wright brothers, you couldn't sustain flight for very long. Flat will glide, but it will not soar.

The reason jets can fly is because their wings are *bent*. By this, I don't mean that the tips curl up or down, but that the top of the wing is thicker in front and curves toward the back, while the bottom of the wing is flat. This is what changes the force in the air and pushes the plane upward.

If I wanted to illustrate this shape with my body, I would kneel with my face to the floor, my back arched and the calves flat on the ground. That's the perfect spiritual shape for faith that flies. It starts with a habitual attitude that demonstrates a humility and willingness to be continuously shaped by God. It's the realization that while we are on this earth, we are a work in progress.

Jeremiah realized this truth one day when God instructed him, *"'Arise and go down to the potter's house, and there I will announce My words to you.'"* The prophet went down to the potter's house and saw him making something out of clay. As the potter's wheel spun around, the vessel he was making was "spoiled," in that it didn't come into shape as the potter originally designed. Instead of throwing out the good clay, the potter made it into something else. The first plan fell apart, so the potter made a new plan. Then God said to Jeremiah, *"Can I not deal with you as this potter does?"*[5]

This pliability enables the Lord to shape us in a way most useful for His purpose. Like an engineer's design that is modified to optimize flight, we must be willing to change in order for God to optimize us. When things don't get off the ground or completely fall apart, we can still allow God to pick us up and make a new plan. However, this demands an attitude of repentance. This is the *bent* that allows us to rise above our failures.

----

[5] *Jeremiah 18:2–6*

Jesus began His public ministry with this word: repent. After being baptized by His cousin, John (who said that his water baptism was for the purpose of repentance), He retreated into the wilderness where He faced temptation as He fasted 40 days and 40 nights. He overcame the temptation and fulfilled Isaiah's prophecy by returning to Capernaum.[6] *"From that time, Jesus began to preach and say, 'Repent, for the kingdom of heaven is at hand'"* (Matthew 4:17).

The Greek word we translate as "repent" is *metanoeo*. It simply means "to change one's mind." Our English word has an overly religious connotation. It feels judgmental and harsh. But all Jesus was saying was essentially, "Get ready to think new thoughts, because God is no longer distant. I am here!" When speaking outside of the church, Christians would probably be better served substituting "repent" with "change your mind." Not only is that clearer to most non-Christians, it conveys a better understanding of this process that we all must undergo.

We all begin from a position of unbelief. Our inborn nature denies the lordship of Christ. Therefore, that needs to be turned around. The crash course we're on must be reversed. True repentance turns that around and enables us to believe. Maintaining a willingness to change our minds when we recognize incorrect thoughts or actions makes us clay in the potter's hand. It's the bend in the wing of belief that pushes us closer to Heaven.

It's too easy to have an emotional experience or join an institution without actually realigning your thoughts with the truth of Christ. We make excuses for our contradictory lifestyle, rationalize our habits, or never pursue God's Word to the point of transformation. This doesn't mean that a truly repentant person will never

<hr />

[6] *Isaiah 9:1, Matthew 4:13–16*

sin; it does mean that true repentance alters our pattern of sin. My pastor likes to say, "You can still sin all you want; you just change your 'want.'" Genuine belief that results in an authentic relationship with a Holy God greatly diminishes the desire to sin. Doing so creates an inherent tension between the indwelling Holy Spirit and the sinful flesh. Sin loses its power because it no longer remains desirable. Repentance thwarts the sinful desires that remain.

Jesus said that we will perish unless we repent.[7] This change of heart and mind results in eternal life. In the book of Acts, Peter preached, *"Therefore repent and return, so that your sins may be wiped away . . . "* (3:19). Repentance is the mechanism that initiates belief; an ongoing attitude of repentance enables it to continue being shaped.

The complimentary attitude to repentance is submission, which is surrendering control to another. It's human nature to pretend that we are in control of our lives. Certainly, we must maintain a level of self-control. After all, it is one sign that the Holy Spirit is influencing our lives. But life is too big for any one of us to handle alone. Any number of things can wreck our sense of control. An unwanted divorce reveals one's helplessness. A tornado or hurricane can quickly overwhelm us. A tragic accident, debilitating illness, or sudden death in the family can devastate. All of these things demonstrate the fact that we don't have as much control as we might wish. Submitting to God puts us under the control of the One who controls it all. That's a much stronger, more hopeful place to be.

Every pilot, regardless of his rank in the cockpit, must submit to the control tower. When they tell him to go up, he goes up.

....
[7] *Luke 13:5*

When they say to bank left, he banks left. The pilot who ignores the control tower quickly gets himself into trouble and puts all of the passengers at risk.

James put it succinctly. *"Submit therefore to God"* (James 4:7). As my pastor also likes to say, "When we see the word 'therefore,' we must ask what it's there for." In verses 1–6, James talks about all of the negative things going on in the world. He mentions quarreling, covetousness, pride, murder, and evil passions. He says that *"friendship with the world is enmity with God."* All of these things bring terrible storms into our lives. It causes us to fight against the Holy Spirit that dwells in us as believers.

The remedy for these destructive things is, therefore, submission to God. That means trading our selfish desires for His desires. It means listening to the heavenly control tower and allowing God to set our course. This *bent* allows us to receive God's grace, James says, and experience His presence in our lives.

Taking a posture of submission and adopting an attitude of repentance shapes our beliefs according to God's truth, not our own ideas. This is the only way to get that lift in our faith that puts us on a journey to a greater life.

Chapter 4

WEIGHT

Certain natural laws must be overcome in order to achieve flight. The first of these is the weight of the aircraft. Large jets have a massive amount of inherent weight. Getting it off the ground and keeping it in the air are no small feats.

We all come into this world with a great spiritual weight. This too must be overcome in order to reach the heights that God intends us to reach. Our planned journey is supernatural, which literally means "departing from what is usual or normal especially so as to appear to transcend the laws of nature."[1] When we overcome the spiritual weight of this world, we transcend the laws of nature to achieve new heights.

Gravity

Few people get hurt flying; it's hitting the ground too hard that does the most damage. Living the Christian life is harmless, until you run hard into sin.

....
[1] *Merriam-Webster*

As long as we live in this fallen world, we feel the gravitational pull of sin. We can't eliminate it, so the scriptures provide another remedy: die to it. Paul says, *"Even so consider yourselves to be dead to sin, but alive to God in Christ Jesus"* (Romans 6:11). Our relationship to sin is a double negative. *"The wages of sin is death . . . "* (Romans 6:23), so dying to sin brings life. It's interesting to note that killing sin doesn't get rid of it; instead it destroys any power it might hold. In that, it is like the relationship between gravity and flight. An airplane doesn't eliminate gravity; instead it rises above it by overcoming its power.

So how do we destroy sin's power? Consider the case of my sister's gerbil. When we were young, my sister Robin and I both had pet gerbils. Herbie lived in my room under my care; Missy lived in Robin's room. We took care of them, played with them, and occasionally cleaned their cages (usually when the stench was bad enough to draw complaints from our parents.)

One week, Robin was so caught up in school and other activities that she forgot one important aspect of caring for a gerbil: feeding it. She came home from school one afternoon to find Missy lying motionless on her side. Naturally, this brought on a fit of mourning for the dead gerbil. The family assembled in her room, saddened at the death of this rodent and perplexed as to what brought it on. Then my mother asked, "Did you feed her?"

A look of guilt and horror passed across Robin's face. She realized that, in fact, several days passed since she last fed the poor creature. Missy starved to death! This was a traumatic experience for a child, but an important lesson. If you want something to stay alive, you have to feed it!

The converse is true, as well. If you want to kill something, starve it. This is the essence of dying to sin: deny it until it ceases to live within you. In the age of grace, this is often forgotten. *"Are we to continue in sin so that grace may increase?"* Paul asks. *"May it never be!"* he answers. *"How shall we who died to sin still live in it?"* (Romans 6:1–2, paraphrased).

Got a bad habit? Quit nursing it. It will eventually be lost to you. Listen to your words. When they sound negative, cruel, or angry, stop them. Think about what you say, and soon you'll kill off the destructive words and be left with peaceful silence, or even better, words that encourage and heal. Feeling discouraged? Douse it with God's Word, a song of praise, or intense prayer. Don't give any damaging thought room to grow. Don't feed it. Let it die.

If we don't practice this denial of sin in our lives, we will be stuck in an endless cycle of spiritual defeat. We will be like an airplane making runs down the runway, but never rising into the air. This is the reason many Christians never get far in life. They repent, but then flounder as they continue feeding sinful thoughts, emotions, actions, and habits. They rev up their spiritual engines every once in a while, but always back off and return to the gate. Sin is always trying to keep us down. Until its force is overcome, it will continue to make flight impossible.

The one positive role that gravity plays in aerodynamics is that it prevents an airplane from spinning out of control. If there was no force reigning in the upward motion of the craft, it would fly so high that it would drift into outer space. The one positive reminder that sin can provide in our lives is the remembrance that we were once slaves to it, but now we are free. Anyone who bears the scars of sin simply needs to look at their own lives to understand how much better off they are without it and how good God is to deliver us from it.

Recalling our former condition should also keep our pride in check. Jesus said in a story to His followers, *"Two men went up into the temple to pray, one a Pharisee and the other a tax collector. The Pharisee stood and was praying this to himself: "God, I thank You that I am not like other people: swindlers, unjust, adulterers, or even like this tax collector. I fast twice a week; I pay tithes of all that I get." But the tax collector, standing some distance away, was even unwilling to lift up his eyes to heaven, but was beating his breast, saying, "God, be merciful to me, the sinner!" I tell you, this man went to his house justified rather than the other; for everyone who exalts himself will be humbled, but he who humbles himself will be exalted."* (Luke 18:10–14).

We must not be bound by sin, but the gravity of our sin should keep us humble. It is only then that we will be exalted, lifted up, and raised high. Through it all, we should remember that success is not of our own making, but only because of the grace, mercy, and forgiveness of Jesus Christ.

Sin is no longer our master, so we should live like freed men. Our past is forgiven, so we should not carry shame. But we also must not become filled with pride. Rather, we must be grateful to the One who has freed us from sin, be diligent to avoid its pull, and praise God for the grace in which we walk.

Paul wrote about this dynamic to a young pastor in Crete named Titus. *"He saved us, not on the basis of deeds which we have done in righteousness, but according to His mercy,"* Paul wrote, reinforcing the truth that salvation comes only by God's grace, not by our good works. He continued to explain that salvation comes *"by the washing of regeneration and renewing by the Holy Spirit, whom He poured out upon us richly through Jesus Christ our Savior, so that being justified by His grace we would be made heirs according to the hope of eternal life"* (Titus 3:5–7).

The ability to escape sin's deadly hold comes only through Christ. Through His grace we become children of the King for eternity. That starts now, if we will allow the Spirit to live and destroy the power of sin. We can overcome sin in this life. It really is possible to rise above it as we are washed and renewed in Him.

Load

Do you want to know if you're worthy to come to God on your own? Compare your life to God's law in the Old Testament, or even the summarized laws of Christ to love God with all your heart, soul, and strength, and love your neighbor as yourself.[2] Are you able to do that on your own? Of course not. We are all human, which means our innate nature always fails when held accountable to God's law. No matter how hard you try, you're not good enough. The law proves it.

The Boeing 777-300ER weighs 370,000 pounds when it is empty. Add fuel, food, luggage, people, and everything else we need for a comfortable journey and it can take off with as much as 775,000 pounds. That's more than the weight of 50 full-grown elephants!

In any discussion about Christianity, the law is the massive elephant in the room. Many of the Old Testament rules are strange and perplexing. Even embarrassing. When taken at face value, they are an immense weight. Paul knew this, which is why he wrote extensively about it. He knew that the weight of the law must be overcome in order for our faith to soar. If we ignore that weight

....
[2] *Luke 10:27*

or do not take it into account, we will be stuck on the ground or, much worse, stall in midair and come crashing down.

On our own, we can do this about as well as elephants can fly, yet people seem to keep trying. Do this, do that; don't do this, don't do that. The list is endless. But Jesus Christ had a different approach. He wrecked a lot of conventional thinking when He walked the earth. In a culture that was used to the conditional rules of "do this to earn God's favor," He basically said that no matter what you do, you will still fall short. After the Sermon on the Mount, He pointed out that He hadn't come to get rid of the Old Testament law, but to fulfill it. He then said, *". . . Unless your righteousness surpasses that of the scribes and Pharisees, you will not enter the kingdom of heaven"* (Matthew 5:20).

Christ's declaration on the load of the law did not eliminate it, but pointed out that it is a load we cannot handle on our own. When it came to the Jewish culture, the scribes and Pharisees were as righteous as it got. Still, that was not enough. But Jesus claimed that He came to fulfill the law. He did what no man could ever do – He lived a perfect life. He fulfilled the part of the Old Covenant the Israelites couldn't keep. Simultaneously, the promise of the Old Covenant – that of a Messiah – was also fulfilled by Him. Because that covenant has been made complete in Christ, we no longer live under those rules. If we tried, we would be utter failures, hopeless, and lost.

Paul expanded in detail on this truth. He repeatedly wrote to various churches and believers to explain that the law is sufficient to point out our insufficiencies, but unable to justify us in the eyes of a Holy God.

"Therefore, my brethren, you also were made to die to the Law through the body of Christ, that you might be joined to another, to Him who was raised from the dead, that we might bear fruit for God."

Romans 7:4

The point of dying to the law is not lawlessness. The load doesn't go away. Instead, we move beyond obedience to a set of rules to the point of truly living a life led by the Spirit – one with peace, love, joy, patience, kindness, and other manifestations of His presence. Fealty to a set of rules was never the point. The Old Testament law was a set of guidelines to push mankind in the right direction, which is righteousness. In and of itself, it is not righteousness. It was the old pathway, but a Spirit-led life is the new (and better) pathway. The load is there, but the work of Christ renders it powerless by overcoming it.

Paul expounded upon the law and its purpose in his first letter to his understudy, Timothy:

"But the goal of our instruction is love from a pure heart and a good conscience and a sincere faith. For some men, straying from these things, have turned aside to fruitless discussion, wanting to be teachers of the Law, even though they do not understand either what they are saying or the matters about which they make confident assertions. But we know that the Law is good, if one uses it lawfully, realizing the fact that law is not made for a righteous person, but for those who are lawless and rebellious, for the ungodly and sinners, for the unholy and profane, for those who kill their fathers or mothers, for murderers and immoral men and homosexuals

*and kidnappers and liars and perjurers, and whatever else is
contrary to sound teaching . . . "*

1 Timothy 1:5–10

Once we become true believers, the law should be dead to us because His righteousness takes us to a place where it simply doesn't apply. When love becomes our all-encompassing motivation, we enter a place beyond the law. But for those who do not believe, the law is still necessary.

In a society without crime, no laws are necessary. Murder is still wrong – even a crime – but if it doesn't exist, the law for it is moot. The laws governing and punishing murderers have no bearing on me because I am not a murderer. I don't live under the penalty of those laws because, in that regard, I am not one of "those who are lawless." Obviously, there is no society without crime, so certain laws are necessary for civil purposes, but God desires His children to live in a way that surpasses mere civil laws.

Consider the practice of abortion. Anyone who actually believes that life begins at conception or implantation would never consider an abortion. To them, it is murder. However, to those who believe life doesn't begin until birth or who don't value life in the womb, abortion is simply birth control. Given that modern science clearly proves that life begins well before birth, it's most likely that abortion advocates simply don't comprehend the value of life in the womb (as opposed to being pre-meditated murderers). Following the logic of Paul, laws are necessary to protect those children who are at risk of abortion. However, those laws would be irrelevant if society understood the value of life and never considered abortion a legitimate course of action. So while laws protecting children in the womb are good, because they are being used in accordance with God's law, the better alternative is knowing that abortion is wrong and never considering it an option. We could outlaw abortion, but those who advocate abortion still need a transformation of the heart and enlightenment of the conscience.

Believers die to the law through the spiritual rebirth required for salvation, which mirrors Christ's death and resurrection, and move beyond righteousness through legislation to justification in Christ. The law should rightly bring us to a point of death to sin, so that we can be reborn into a life of fruitful living. Without the law, we wouldn't necessarily know how sinful we are. But when we compare our lives to God's definition of right and wrong, we see how badly we need a Savior. It is then not our righteousness that leads to salvation, but the righteousness of Christ, of which we partake.

> *"For through the Law I died to the Law, so that I might live to God. I have been crucified with Christ; and it is no longer I who live, but Christ lives in me; and the life which I now live in the flesh I live by faith in the Son of God, who loved me and gave Himself up for me."*
>
> Galatians 2:19–20

I find it interesting that the law was given to Moses on a mountain and Jesus said that faith can move a mountain. Our faith, that genuine, active belief in Jesus Christ, moves that mountain of the law and gives us life. The Spirit should lead us, not a set of rules. In this, righteous living is no longer a burden, but a joy. An airplane with adequate power is not dragged down by the weight of its contents. Likewise, a believer with the power of the Holy Spirit will not be dragged down by the weight of the law.

Mass

A similar aeronautical concern that compliments weight is mass. Technically, mass measures how much matter is in an object while weight measures how hard gravity pulls on that object. Dying to the law reduces the pull of sin, but there's still the issue of how much matter is in the object. Spiritually, we are the matter. That is, the more we live for self, the greater our "mass" brings us down.

In the final days leading up to Christ's crucifixion, He told His disciples:

> *"Truly, truly, I say to you, unless a grain of wheat falls into the earth and dies, it remains alone; but if it dies, it bears much fruit. He who loves his life loses it, and he who hates his life in this world will keep it to life eternal."*
>
> John 12:24–25

He was foreshadowing His own death and resurrection, while conveying a universal truth: You cannot truly live the Christian life until you die to yourself. For Christ, that meant literal death; but since He became the final sacrifice and fulfilled the requirements of the law once and for all, we do not have to face the same physical death. However, we must die to the selfish desires that interfere with our new life in Christ.

We wonder why people come into the church, say a wonderful prayer or have a great experience, then fall into devastating sin. Often, it's because their flesh is still alive and well. Churches can even be guilty of pushing immature believers into positions of leadership or stardom. Really, what we should be encouraging is a thorough death of self, which will then lead to a fruitful Christian life.

Simply "coming to Christ" does not achieve this. The rich young ruler came to Christ, but walked away because he couldn't die to his love of money and possessions. When Jesus told him to sell everything he had, give it to the poor, and then follow Him, the man left saddened. He wanted to follow Christ, but couldn't let go of his worldly possessions. So he came and went.

Judas Iscariot spent years close to Christ, but never died to his own ambitions. He betrayed Jesus because he pursued his own, selfish course. Truly following Christ means abandoning our own desires and replacing them with His.

Frederick Brotherton Meyer (1847–1929), the great English pastor and friend of Dwight L. Moody, wrote, "Most of us are too strong for Him to use; we are too full of our own schemes, and plans, and ways of doing things. He must empty us, and humble us, and bring us down to the dust of death, so low that we need every straw of encouragement, every leaf of help; and then He will raise us up, and make us as the rod of His strength."

It's hard to lay down our ambitions. It's much easier to dress them up in spiritual lingo and justify them. But God calls us to empty ourselves completely so that He can fill us up. It's the sentiment John the Baptist expressed when he said, *"He must increase, but I must decrease"* (John 3:30). God doesn't come into our lives to give us a hand, but to take over. We are not partners; He is the Potter and we are the clay. He is the Father and we are His children. Obedience to His will is non-negotiable. Struggling against this reality amounts to spiritual frustration and hinders us from living life in full.

Too many of us want to skip straight to the resurrection without experiencing the cross. But there is no new life without death, and death isn't partial, it's whole. Paul said, *"Now those who belong to Christ Jesus have crucified the flesh with its passions and desires"* (Galatians 5:24). This "flesh" is us – not literal flesh, but the passions and desires that are ours and not God's. They need not even be bad things by human standards, but merely those things that are not exclusively God's will for our lives. You may want to be a missionary in Africa, but if God has called you to run a small business that glorifies Him in the way you treat your employees and serve your customers, pursuing anything else amounts to selfish disobedience.

My sons and I have a special bonding moment each Sunday night. We watch *The Walking Dead* together. It's ridiculous – infected people coming back to life to feed on human flesh – but it's fun. I think it may be inspired by some people in the church – those whose flesh won't die, so they stagger around in confusion, muttering incomprehensible things and frightening everyone else. There is nothing attractive or inspiring about people who hold on to their rotting flesh. It stinks. They are of little or no use to anyone.

Like Lazarus, who literally died and was raised back to life, we cannot experience new life in Christ until we figuratively die. We must be freed from the flesh, *"for if you are living according to the flesh, you must die; but if by the Spirit you are putting to death the deeds of the body, you will live"* (Romans 8:13).

Dying to self reduces the mass of "me" and allows more of Him. The goal is to completely lose ourselves in Christ to the point that people clearly see Him in us. This is the beauty of John the Baptist's declaration, *"He must increase, but I must decrease"* (John 3:30). With every lessening of ourselves, we rise a little higher.

Chapter 5 ··

DRAG

In aerodynamics, *drag* is the force opposing an object as it moves through the air. It slows an object down and makes it inefficient for flight. The larger the surface area, the more the *drag*. Similarly, there are several forces that can drag us down, making us less effective in this world. That's why Paul instructed us to *"lay aside every encumbrance and the sin which so easily entangles us."*[1] The Greek word for "encumbrance" means "bulk, mass, and burden." Eradicating these burdens eliminates the forces opposing our forward progress.

Resistance

Have you ever wondered why commercial jets typically fly at around 35,000 feet? It's because the air is thinner at that altitude, which means there is less resistance. Simply put, they fly that high because it's easier and more efficient.

················

[1] *Hebrews 12:1*

Life is always easier when we have less resistance, but resistance has a purpose. Do you know why most airplanes don't fly at 50,000 or 60,000 feet? If there is less resistance the higher you go, why not go even higher? The answer is that when the air thins too much, the average airplane can't maintain its direction. A lack of resistance causes it to "skate" in the sky, unable to keep moving forward in a straight line. It would roll and flounder, eventually falling.

Resistance helps us maintain focus. It forces us to work for what we want. At the same time, it can also frustrate us and prevent us from moving forward properly. The key to knowing how to deal with resistance comes from developing spiritual sensitivity.

"Beloved, do not believe every spirit, but test the spirits to see whether they are from God, because many false prophets have gone out into the world" (1 John 4:1). When we find resistance from people, we must ask: *Is this helping to keep me in line or hindering God's purpose?* I think the hardest part about this is the fact that people can quickly go in and out of God's will unintentionally and without warning. As believers, we must have our spiritual "radars" up at all times. That doesn't mean operating with extreme suspicion or viewing everyone pessimistically. It means having sensitivity to the spirit operating within someone else to know if it is perfectly in line with God's purpose for us or not. This, of course, requires us to be honest about the spirit operating within ourselves. If our radar is corrupt, we won't be able to tell where others are in life. But when we are aligned with the Holy Spirit, we can learn to tell whether others are in line as well.

Consider the case of the disciple Simon Peter (called bar-Jona, or son of Jonah). He answers Jesus' question about His identity with, *"'You are the Christ, the Son of the living God.' And Jesus said to him, 'Blessed are you, Simon Barjona, because flesh and blood did not reveal this to you, but My Father who is in heaven'"* (Matthew 16:16–17). That's just about the highest compliment one can get! Simon Peter was perfectly aligned with the Holy Spirit in that moment. But then Jesus foretells His abuse and crucifixion in Jerusalem and *"Peter took Him aside and began to rebuke Him, saying, 'God forbid it, Lord! This shall never happen to You.'"* This time, he was out of line. His spiritual sensitivity faltered even though just a few minutes prior he was speaking from the mouth of God. Jesus' reply is not so complimentary this time. *"'Get behind Me, Satan!'"* (Matthew 16:22–23).

If the apostle we hold up as one of the greatest witnesses of all time can slip that fast, then what about your spouse, friend, or pastor? Again, the correct response is not cynicism or suspicion, but finely tuned spiritual sensitivity. It puts the onus on each of us individually to be tuned to the Holy Spirit instead of merely relying on others we regard as "more spiritual." In Peter's case, Jesus elaborated on His "get behind Me" statement by saying, *"'You are not setting your mind on God's interests, but man's'"* (v23). It's quite telling that "man's interests" are tied to Satan. Peter's resistance to Christ was not overtly satanic, but demonstrably human – he didn't want to see Christ suffer. But perhaps that's the point: Anything that is not from God is from Satan. What may appear to be some harmless human interest has to either line up with God's plan or not, so there's no middle ground. There is only what is of God and what is not of God. A major part of our growth as believers is learning to tell the difference between the two. That is spiritual sensitivity.

If you look at the back of a plane, you see a trio of fixed pieces. They look like a vertical tail and two short horizontal wings. These are called *stabilizers*, and they keep the rest of the plane from swinging up, down, right, or left. Without *stabilizers*, airplanes cannot fly straight. They would dangerously change direction without warning. The stabilizer in our lives is the Word of God. Studying, meditating, and understanding the Bible keeps us stable, preventing wild swings in thought or attitude. If you've ever known someone who drifted into serious error following things that are clearly unscriptural, you've probably witnessed them veering off course or vacillating wildly in their faith. When we begin to doubt the veracity of God's Word, we become terribly unstable. James describes it this way:

> *"But if any of you lacks wisdom, let him ask of God, who gives to all generously and without reproach, and it will be given to him. But he must ask in faith without any doubting, for the one who doubts is like the surf of the sea, driven and tossed by the wind. For that man ought not to expect that he will receive anything from the Lord, being a double-minded man, unstable in all his ways."*
>
> James 1:5–8

Notice that James says to ask God for wisdom. He wants to give it to us. He does not want us to flounder and roll in mid-air. He will hone our sensitivity to Him when we continually come to Him with things. When we face resistance in our lives, we take it to Him and ask for wisdom. He will help us determine where it's coming from and whether it has a purpose. We can check it against His Word to stabilize our decisions. We can then respond in a way that moves us closer to His purposes. That way, any type of resistance works in our favor, whether to push us in a better direction or cause us to become more resilient to fight through it.

There's an interesting passage when Jesus sent His disciples out to witness for Him. He told them, *"Whoever does not receive you, nor heed your words, as you go out of that house or that city, shake the dust off your feet"* (Matthew 10:14). He was essentially saying, "If you meet resistance, move on."

In Acts 16, Paul was trying to preach the gospel through regions of modern Turkey when the Holy Spirit prevented him from entering an area and directed him to what is now Greece.[2] It would have been logical for Paul to think, *The people in Bithynia and Troas need to hear the gospel, so I must go there.* But God resisted his plans and moved him elsewhere.

Resistance will occur. Determining its purpose and responding correctly to it will keep us moving in the right direction. Spiritual sensitivity will help us know whether to respond by making adjustments or pushing the throttle forward.

Shape

The primary cause of negative *drag* in aeronautics is the shape of the aircraft. Flight means moving an object through air, which has density. Just as the right shape enables an airplane to get lift, the wrong shape creates *drag* that, when it reaches a certain point, prevents flight altogether.

When we claim to believe something, but think and act differently, it creates a spiritual drag that holds us back. One of my favorite verses, and lifelong prayers, comes from Jesus' encounter with a man whose son suffered from seizures. They brought the boy to Him and he fell to the ground, convulsing and foaming at the mouth. Jesus asked the father, "How long has this been

[2] *Acts 16:6–12*

happening to him?" The father answered, "From childhood. It has often thrown him both into the fire and into the water to destroy him. But if You can do anything, take pity on us and help us!"

Jesus tested the man with His response. "'If You can?'" He said. It's almost as if Jesus was surprised at the man's conditional statement. The father said, "if." "If?" Jesus replied. Then He put it back on the man by saying, "All things are possible to him who believes."

The father's response is one I completely understand. It may be paradoxical, but in our human state, it makes perfect sense. "I do believe," he replied, "help my unbelief!"[3]

Unbelief is a drag. It's a shape that reduces our lift. So we must check our claims of faith against the way we think and act. Unbelief is usually accompanied by thoughts like, *That's not what the Bible really means* or *Nobody will know.* It can be ignorance or willful dismissal, but either way, it works against our ability to effectively operate.

A friend and I were skiing at Keystone in Colorado one winter. The snow wasn't very good that year, so many trails were closed. We came upon one such trail in the middle of the mountain. Trails all around it were open, but this one was roped off with a very legible "Trail Closed" sign hanging on the rope. Yet we could clearly see the trail on the other side, and it was covered with snow. And not just any snow, but beautiful, unbroken powder.

My friend (we'll call him "John" because that's his name and this whole debacle was totally his fault) suggested we experience the wonder of such powder. I pointed out that the trail was closed for a reason. "Look at that powder!" he exclaimed as he cut under the rope. I couldn't disagree. It was the best snow we'd seen. So I

....
[3] *Mark 9:17–24*

followed. For several minutes, we enjoyed the best run we had all day. It was perfect: clear skies above and untested powder below.

And then it ended.

We came to a steep bank that was more rocks than snow – and it was a long way down. Thick trees on each side made it impossible to go around. There was only one way out and it was ugly. I made it halfway on skis before running completely out of snow. I had to take off my skis and walk the rest of the way down – no easy task on a steep, slick incline in ski boots. By the time I made it, I was exhausted and had a deep gash on one ski. All because I didn't believe the warning sign. Sure, I knew better. I know that the ski patrol checks the mountain every day and only closes dangerous trails. I don't think I actually know the mountain better than they do. I just listened to the wrong voice and chose to believe something that wasn't true.

If I wasn't an experienced skier, I might not know better. Yet ignorance of the truth doesn't change the outcome. I still would have found myself at the wrong end of a steep and treacherous drop. That's why it's important to know the truth, believe it, and act on it.

We obviously made it out all right. Laughed about it, in fact. But it illustrates an important point. Unbelief gets us into trouble. Sometimes we manage to walk out relatively unscathed, but not always. And the more we press the limits of this form of rebellion, the greater our odds of causing irreparable damage. Unbelief is a shape that simply won't fly.

Let's say that you're waiting at the airport to go somewhere. A man in an official-looking uniform walks up to you and tells you that the terminal is being evacuated because of a bomb threat.

Now, consider these three statements and assume one of them is absolutely true:

1. The man works for the Transportation Safety Authority.
2. The man's uniform is phony and he is a compulsive liar.
3. You are being pranked and your friends are watching on hidden cameras.

Will what you believe impact your response to the man? Of course it will. If he's legitimately warning you, then you'd immediately run for the exit. If he's a nutcase, you'd probably report him to the real authorities. And if he's an actor, you might smile and look around for the cameras.

Of course, that scenario is meaningless to you right now. But what about these?

1. Jesus Christ is the only way to know God.
2. God has a specific purpose and plan for your life.
3. As a believer, you should have peace, joy, patience, self-control, kindness, and love.

Do you believe those things? If you don't, then you really don't believe the Bible. If you do, then it should affect every thought you have and everything you do – as should every other piece of information the Bible presents. This is what Jesus Christ was talking about when He said "believe."

Failing to know the truth or act on it results in self-inflicted *drag* against the higher calling of Christ. I'm not trying to convince you that if you struggle with things, then you don't believe. We all have battles to fight, so take comfort. It's okay to declare, "Lord I believe, help my unbelief!" It's those who don't fight who need to examine their faith.

Parasites

There is a phrase in aeronautics called *parasitic drag*. It is defined as all *drag* that is not associated with the production of lift. The nose of the airplane has a pointed shape to reduce *parasitic drag*. The same is true on military jets that carry missiles and bombs. Those are shaped like a teardrop to reduce the *drag* on the jet. All airplanes are streamlined to avoid the negative pull of *parasitic drag*. Surfaces are even painted, waxed, and cleaned with this in mind.

When we hang on to things that are counterproductive to our spiritual "lift," they amount to be parasites. Harboring resentment, entertaining impure thoughts, puffing ourselves up with pride, and thinking or doing anything that rebuffs the Holy Spirit only serves to fight against the work of Christ. When we are unable to let go of these things on our own, that parasitic grip is called a stronghold.

In 2 Corinthians 10, the New King James Version describes the weapons of spiritual warfare and applies them to strongholds. In the Old Testament, this term denoted a fortress or impenetrable position. In the spiritual context of Paul's writing, he's talking about a stubborn idea or belief. Other translations render this concept as *"strongholds of human reasoning"* (NLT), *"the enemy's strong places"* (NCV), and *"barriers erected against the truth of God"* (MSG).

Strongholds are untrue thoughts that are so deeply rooted that they keep you trapped in wrong actions. They are often accompanied by thoughts of *I can't help it* or *I'll get forgiveness later.* They can become ingrained through hurt, confusion, unforgiveness, bitterness, and other negative emotions or painful experiences.

A pastor's son who is a friend of mine went through a terrible experience with his parents. His father divorced his mother, then married my friend's girlfriend! He was, understandably, quite bitter. He described it with an expletive I won't repeat, but suffice to say he felt that "the whole ministry thing" was a lie. Fortunately for him, he was able to work through that pain, because if that idea had stuck in his head, he would have walked away from God and entered a lonely world of anger and resentment. That singular idea would have caused him to behave in ways he never intended. It would have become an external, parasitic force to drag him down.

I am happy to say that he moved on, found a wonderful wife, started his own family, and now pastors a church. But for many others, wrong ideas lodge. They take hold and ruin lives. A stronghold can only be dislodged by a powerful intervention of the Holy Spirit, possibly with the help of other believers or professional counselors.

There's an interesting passage in the Old Testament that I'd heard many times, but never understood the true implications. *"Where there is no vision, the people perish; but he that keepeth the law, happy is he"* (Proverbs 29:18, NKJV). I had always taken that to mean that when people lack a goal, they die, whether emotionally, spiritually, or literally. But the New American Standard Bible says, *"Where there is no vision, the people are unrestrained . . . "* This is actually more true to the Hebrew and carries a different idea. The term "vision" also means "divine communication." The verb "perish" or "are unrestrained" means "let go," "loosened," and "neglected." When we cease having "divine communication," or the Holy Spirit's active involvement with our thoughts, we neglect our spiritual mindset and let go of the truth. This is the perfect recipe for a stronghold.

Proverbs 28:13–14 says, *"He who conceals his transgressions will not prosper, but he who confesses and forsakes them will find compassion. How blessed is the man who fears always, but he who hardens his heart will fall into calamity."*

There is healing in confessing our negative thoughts, damaged emotions, and difficult struggles to God, and sometimes to others. Hiding it causes us to become numb to the sin. Jesus said we have eyes, but don't see; ears, but don't hear. This insensitivity to our own harmful thoughts and actions keeps us enslaved to them. But notice that confession is only the first step to finding compassion. The rest of the solution lies in forsaking them. That means walking away and abandoning them. We recognize them, then run from them. Just admitting that something is wrong does not complete the process of breaking down the stronghold. Once a prison door is unlocked, we must walk out.

Here's another interesting thing about *parasitic drag*: the interference it causes is not an additional hindrance, but one that is compounded. In other words, if an airplane's speed doubles, the *drag* of the parasite doesn't merely double, it quadruples. There is naturally induced *drag* any time an airplane attempts to fly, but *parasitic drag* exerts stronger resistance than normal.

Any time we walk with God, there is natural resistance in this fallen world, but if we have a stronghold, it will exert a compounded pull. For example, the man who becomes a pastor, but holds onto lust in his heart will find that stronghold compounding as he expands his ministry. As his influence increases, the stronghold doesn't decrease; instead it pulls more fiercely. These things cannot be ignored. That's why we must *"lay aside every encumbrance and the sin which so easily entangles us."*[4]

The process in aeronautics is called *fairing* or *filleting*. It's the smoothing of surfaces to reduce drag. Spiritually, it's called *pruning*. Jesus said every branch that bears fruit, He prunes it so that it may

....
[4] *Hebrews 12:1*

bear more fruit (John 15:2b). He will streamline us so that we're free from *parasitic drag*. It's an ongoing process of maintenance and improvement that requires us to abide in His presence with a willingness to learn and heed correction. At the same time, it invites an act on our part to intentionally "lay aside" those things that drag us down. That's the "forsaking" that the Psalmist noted. Identify the parasite and get rid of it.

Eliminating strongholds drastically improves our ability to rise higher, maintain our course, and fly further. We really don't need those worldly parasites. Allowing the Holy Spirit to routinely smooth out our rough edges significantly increases our ability to soar in Him. As those encumbrances cease to have an effect on our daily living, our journey becomes easier and our impact on others grows stronger.

Chapter 6

THRUST

Anyone who has ever flown has felt that moment when the engines rev up and begin hurling you down the runway. The rumble of power provides the necessary thrust to enable the precisely-shaped wings to overcome the inherent weight and opposing *drag* to lift the plane off the ground. At this point, the plane has been properly prepared to use the power of the engines in order to rise and fly.

In the life of a true believer who has accepted the truth of Jesus Christ and died to sin and the law, the new things that take over provide the necessary thrust to rise above this world. Until this God-enabled fuel is ignited in our hearts and minds, we will never possess the power to propel our faith beyond mediocre. As we become more of the person God created us to be, we are able to do things previously unattainable. Paul calls you a "new creature." Out of your previous sinful nature, God creates a new person through your faith in Jesus Christ. These new characteristics carry us on the journey He intends us to complete.

Fuel

Every time an airplane lands, it refuels. Otherwise, it will stay on the ground. It doesn't matter how masterfully the plane is designed, how powerful the engines are, or how skilled the pilots may be, without fuel, it goes nowhere. A plane may be capable of flying around the world and back, but it constantly needs to be refueled.

In the same way, we need spiritual fuel on a daily basis. It doesn't matter how strong our faith may be or how much we may have achieved in the past, when we quit taking in fuel, we end up stuck on the ground. God tried to teach this lesson to the Israelites with the daily dose of manna. It wouldn't last more than one day because God wanted them to trust Him anew each morning. Jesus prayed, *"Give us this day our daily bread"* (Matthew 6:11). He didn't say "enough on Sunday to get us through the week." We must learn to fellowship with Him every day, from our waking moment until we drift off to sleep at night. Every day requires refueling with a full supply of His presence, guidance, and wisdom.

What exactly does that look like? Naturally, things like prayer and reading the Bible are a part of that, but I think it goes to something deeper. The real fuel in our lives comes from not merely being a hearer of His Word, but a doer.

Jesus said, *"If you love Me, you will keep My commandments"* (John 14:15). Note the order there. We love Christ, then we keep His commandments. We've seen that in Him we are dead to the law, so this is not a test to prove our love for Him. Instead, it is the natural course of action for those who love Him. An obedient lifestyle comes through devotion. A loyal slave or child will do what his master or father instructs out of duty. But Jesus Christ takes us to a place beyond fealty and into friendship.

He said, *"You are My friends if you do what I command you. No longer do I call you slaves, for the slave does not know what his master is doing; but I have called you friends, for all things that I have heard from My Father I have made known to you"* (John 15:14–15).

That's an amazing paradigm shift. We offer ourselves as slaves, receive adoption as sons and daughters, and become *friends* with the Creator of the universe! Because of the myriad of jacked-up relationships among people, and often with fathers, we tend to look at God through the tainted lens of human interaction. Children who've been abandoned tend to see God as detached. Women who have been abused often view God as uncaring or unjust. Those brought up in a legalistic home usually view God as some cosmic avenger, itching to punish us for our wrongdoings. But Jesus Christ plainly said that He wants to be our friend.

The Greek word *philos* has the connotation not only of friendship, but companionship. In our Facebook world, it's easy to have a wide circle of "friends" who we really don't know very well or spend much time with. But the scriptural context of Christ's is that He is not a casual acquaintance, but someone we hang out with. That means spending time with Him, talking to Him, and listening. When that happens, He tells us things and shows us things. He did it with His disciples and He continues to do it today for those who spend time in the presence of the Holy Spirit. This not only makes it easier to know His will for our lives, but much more exciting to actually do it. Obedience becomes fun!

The Jesus Culture song *I Want To Know You* contains an interesting phrase: "I give You my worship / All of my passion." Have you ever considered giving God your passion? I don't mean that in a romantic way, but in the way that one might have a passion for sports, family, or success. Consider how you invest the majority of your time and energy – not those the things required of you, but the things you enjoy. What would happen if you gave your most passionate energy to the mission of knowing God and helping others know Him? I dare say it would change things drastically.

The English word "enthusiasm" comes from the Greek words *en* and *theos,* meaning "God in us." Obedience that is not discipline but an enthusiastic passion has far more power and joy. This is the place to which we must strive. It's the place the Holy Spirit longs to take us.

Those who attend church begrudgingly, perform good works out of guilt, or do any other righteous act with negative feelings lack enthusiasm because God is not in their hearts. King David understood this, and after experiencing the grace, forgiveness, and power of God in his life, he was able to honestly proclaim, *"'I delight to do Your will, O my God; Your Law is within my heart'"* (Psalm 40:8).

Obedience shouldn't be a burden. If it is, then you may need to check the shape of your belief to make sure it lines up with the word and character of God. You may need to be washed in His grace, love, and power so that you comprehend the joy in knowing and doing His will. Then you can enthusiastically obey, because God is in you and your delight is in Him. This enthusiasm is the fuel that makes flight possible and gives us the strength to do it daily.

Power

As I climbed the long brick stairway and passed statues of multi-headed dragons and stone guardians bearing swords, I wondered what evil spirits awaited me in the grand Wot Penh. The ornate Buddhist temple stands on the highest hill in the capital city of Cambodia, and with a few hours to kill before beginning a trip into the interior of the country to gather interviews of girls rescued from sex trafficking and stories of families decimated by filthy drinking water, I decided to visit this famous tourist site and place of worship for faithful Buddhists.

Monks garbed in bright orange robes quietly wandered the grounds. Vendors sold birds to be released for good luck. Altars of incense reminded worshippers to pursue good conduct and moral purity. At the pinnacle where the great golden Buddha sits inside the heart of the temple, I slipped off my shoes and stood in the back as others knelt and offered prayers to the statue. Some brought fruit to be offered to the monks while others lit incense or placed flowers around the fat, smiling figure. Traditional music filled the room as I pondered the spiritual ramifications of their sincere acts of piety. I felt nothing. No tangible presence of anything good or evil. Just a cold, lifeless room with beautiful paint and shimmering gold. It was a glamorous tomb.

A few days later, as I stood with a Cambodian family at the grave of their child who had died of dysentery after drinking from the local water source, the mother told me, "We prayed to Buddha and nothing happened." No wonder, because Buddha, no matter how kind or well-meaning he may have been, is dead.

This is empty religion. It is dead. It offers nothing. No matter how earnest its followers may be, it is powerless to do anything. Good intentions and sincere prayers go nowhere. The stone statues are as dead as its founders.

Paul told the church at Corinth, *"I determined to know nothing among you except Jesus Christ . . . and my message and my preaching were not in persuasive words of wisdom, but in demonstration of the Spirit and of power, so that your faith would not rest on the wisdom of men, but on the power of God"* (1 Corinthians 2:2, 4–5).

Believers must demonstrate this power, bearing in mind that it is not something we conjure up through our own will, wisdom, or works. God's power flows freely when we stop bottling it up. It's not something we create, but rather something we release. Our *"cup overflows"*(Psalm 23:5). Every time a jumbo jet leaves the runway, it is a demonstration of power. Fuel combusts in the engines, the systems work in harmony with each other, and the forces of nature must yield to the desire of the pilot because of the power generated by the airplane. When we walk in obedience to the Spirit and boldly carry our faith into the world, the natural forces that resist us must yield to the supernatural power of God. This is true because of the truth of Christ's resurrection. His tomb is empty. The cross is not just a symbol, but the intersection of the horizontal and vertical where the corruption of this natural world must yield to power of His supernatural grace.

Jesus exuded power when He walked the earth. When He first gathered the twelve disciples, a crowd followed Him and *"all the people were trying to touch Him, for power was coming from Him and healing them all"* (Luke 6:19). After His resurrection, He appeared to His apostles, saying, *". . . you will receive power when the Holy Spirit has come upon you . . . "* (Acts 1:8). This empowerment was recorded in the next chapter, and the church exploded in number and influence.

Paul later wrote to the gentiles in Rome, *"For I am not ashamed of the gospel, for it is the power of God for salvation to everyone who believes, to the Jew first and also to the Greek"* (Romans 1:16). That power did not pass away with the early church, but continues today. *"Now to Him who is able to do far more abundantly beyond all that we ask or think, according to the power that works within us, to Him be the glory in the church and in Christ Jesus to all genera-tions forever and ever"* (Ephesians 3:20–21).

This is the power of Christ. It has been saving people for 2,000 years and will continue for those who believe in Him. It exceeds our ability to comprehend it *"beyond all that we ask or think."* It is not only available, but essential. Without it, you cannot overcome the forces that seek to hold you down. But with it, you can *"fulfill every desire for goodness and the work of faith with power, so that the name of our Lord Jesus will be glorified in you, and you in Him"* (2 Thessalonians 1:11–12).

Rick Warren, author of *The Purpose-Driven Life*, wrote, "Your obedience in moving forward – to take risks and step out in faith – will release God's power in your life."[1] Obedience fuels God's power. It ignites the Holy Spirit. Becoming a doer of His Word makes things happen. It's not generating something of our own will, but, as Pastor Warren said, releasing His will in our lives and in the lives of others. It's the manifestation of Jesus' prayer, *"'Your kingdom come. Your will be done, on earth as it is in heaven'"* (Matthew 6:10).

Religions may simulate flight, but without the power of the risen One, there is no force for real change. It's easy for us to underestimate the power of Christ in our lives by overestimating the power of things we see. We rely too heavily on the government to enforce morality, blame the devil for our troubles, look to wealth to enable us, bemoan the past and worry about the future, place our hopes in people, and fear sickness and death. But the power those things have pales in comparison to the power of God's grace and love. This is where we should focus our time, resources, and

....
[1] *http://purposedriven.com/blogs/dailyhope/index.html?contentid=5575*

energy. If we want to live a life of power, we must respond more to His voice than anything else. This is our source of life.

Paul wrote, *"For I am convinced that neither death, nor life, nor angels, nor principalities, nor things present, nor things to come, nor powers, nor height, nor depth, nor any other created thing, will be able to separate us from the love of God, which is in Christ Jesus our Lord"* (Romans 8:38–39). This is power – real power – and He wants to release it in you.

Constancy

Once an airplane reaches cruising altitude, the thrusters are pared back a bit, but they are not shut down. Obviously, that would be a really bad idea. For flight to continue, the thrusters must be constantly engaged.

Many believers experience a great thrust of power when they come to Christ. The change that takes place can be so radical that it creates a kind of adrenaline rush. When life settles into a more consistent pace, it's easy to allow two terrible tendencies to throttle our thrust to dangerously low levels.

The first is apathy. This comes with thoughts like, *I deserve to do what I want* or *It doesn't really matter.* This is perhaps the most dangerous expression of bad thinking, since you don't do what you claim to believe because you just don't care.

My wife never gained much weight when pregnant with any of our four children. Every time, she bounced back to her normal, healthy self a few months after giving birth. I, on the other hand, wasn't so lucky. I gained about 10 pounds per child. All four were born within five-and-a-half years, and after our family was complete, I kept on gaining. My sedentary lifestyle contributed to the weight gain, but the primary factor was my diet. I was working for a Fortune 500 company, then a dot-com startup, and I was part of the office crew that went out to lunch every day. We ate well. Too well. Fried chicken strips with honey mustard and fries. Pizza buffets. Thick, greasy hamburgers. Lots of Mexican food.

The problem was that I didn't care. I knew my weight, and by extension my life, was out of control. I knew it was wrong. I could talk a great game about diet and exercise, but I wasn't living it. I didn't lack for knowledge, just motivation. Apathy was slowly killing me, physically and spiritually.

We have a fabulous family photo hanging above the stairs. I love it and hate it. The kids are adorable at ages two, four, six, and eight. I look like a walrus. At the time of the photo, tying my shoes took my breath away. Playing with the kids made me tired. I had to buy bigger clothes. I was not happy.

In my mid-30s I decided I'd had enough. I went hardcore with my diet and exercised every day. It took eight months, but I dropped 50 pounds. No longer did my appetite control me. I finally did the right thing because I cared. That doesn't mean that I never struggle. I put some weight back on when multiple eye surgeries required avoiding strenuous activity. But I fight it. No longer does apathy reign. I truly believe that we should care for our bodies, and I make it a point to act on that belief. Every day that I do the right thing is a small victory.

Spiritual apathy is even more dangerous than indifference about your physical condition. It means the thrusters have shut down and a crash is imminent. One can only glide for so long. This was the message John conveyed in the book of Revelation to the church in Sardis. *"Wake up, and strengthen the things that remain, which were about to die; for I have not found your deeds completed in the sight of My God"* (Revelation 3:2). This ancient church had a reputation of being alive because they looked good on the outside. But most of the people were depleted on the inside. Theologian George Eldon Ladd described the Sardian church as "a picture of nominal Christianity, outwardly prosperous, busy with the externals of religious activity, but devoid of spiritual life and power."[2] This is what happens when apathy reigns. It is the precursor to spiritual death. When the thrusters shut down, a crash is imminent.

There is no good reason to become apathetic about the mission we are on. As long as we are alive, our deeds are not complete. There is always more work for us to do building His Kingdom. When we feel like God is done with us, we must wake up and rediscover His power and purpose. The thrusters must be constantly pushed forward to keep making progress.

The second major problem that can prematurely end a flight is a disruption in the fuel supply. Running out of fuel or temporarily cutting it off results in disaster. We must learn how to replenish our strength on a daily basis.

One of the coolest things in modern military flight is the ability for jets to refuel in mid-air. For believers, this is really what our refueling process looks like, because we don't need to stop in order to maintain our supply.

Twice Paul tells us not to lose heart or grow weary in doing good.[3] Doing good, biblically speaking, is doing the will of God, which is obedience. This does not require perfection. The question is not whether we will fail (we will), but how we respond to our own failure. Do we become exhausted and defeated or do we unclog the fuel lines and continue our journey?

....

[2] *A Commentary on the Revelation of John, p. 56*
[3] *Galatians 6:9, 2 Thessalonians 3:13*

When we make the effort to continually maintain our relationship with Christ and seek to do His will (even when we miss it sometimes), we develop a critical characteristic called dependability. Jesus said to His disciples, *"He who is faithful in a very little thing is faithful also in much; and he who is unrighteous in a very little thing is unrighteous also in much"* (Luke 16:10). We have a great task, but we will never fulfill it if we are not reliable. This works horizontally and vertically. When we live in obedience to God, He trusts us with more. And when we prove to be trustworthy to people, they begin to believe in us as well.

We all know people who are unreliable. We also learn very quickly not to depend on them for certain things. If others perceive us as people who cannot be trusted to act responsibly and do what we say we will do, how can we expect them to listen when we share the Gospel? People must trust our actions before they will trust our words. An unreliable airplane is not allowed to fly. Instead, it is "grounded" while mechanics work to fix the problems. Unreliable people need to get "grounded" in God's Word so that He can repair those things that cause them to be unreliable.

When we prove ourselves trustworthy to God, He puts us in a position to show our faithfulness to others. This is a critical trait for our mission. There is a great reward promised to those who develop dependability. Jesus said, *" . . . You were faithful with a few things, I will put you in charge of many things; enter into the joy of your master"* (Matthew 25:23). Another connotation to the word *pistos*, which is translated in this verse as "faithful," is "one who trusts in God's promises." I don't care how much some pilot promises that his plane is safe, if I don't trust him, I'm not getting on board. Fully understanding that we can depend on God and

His Word enables us to get on board with His plan. Once we're on board, He rewards our trust by taking us higher.

If you really want to experience more spiritually and be entrusted with more from God, then prove yourself faithful in the things already given to you. Stop looking for new things and take care of the existing responsibilities. If you are married, be an amazingly faithful spouse – not just in the fidelity of the marriage, but in the pursuit of oneness with your husband or wife. If you are a parent, be a consistent example of Christ to your children. If you work outside the home, be the most diligent boss or employee the company has ever seen. Whatever God puts before you, take it seriously and excel at it out of faithfulness to Him. Then He will give you more.

Developing the traits of faithfulness, trustworthiness, and dependability really amounts to reflecting the nature of God within our own lives. Because God is faithful, we trust the words and work of Jesus Christ and depend on the Holy Spirit to empower us. Consequently, we become people on whom God can depend to represent Him here on earth. Others learn to trust us as well. This enables us to constantly reach further in our flight of faith.

Chapter 7

CRUISING

Cruise flight is the phase that falls between climb and descent. It is typically the longest phase of the flight. Spiritually, cruising is simply maintaining our walk of faith. It is abiding in Christ without interruption. Paul wrote, *"It was for freedom that Christ set us free; therefore keep standing firm and do not be subject again to a yoke of slavery"* (Galatians 5:1). When we learn to stand firm and avoid the chains of sin, we maintain a healthy cruising altitude. In doing that, we balance three principles related to aeronautics that also provide a lesson for our faith.

Attitude

On July 22, 2013, a Southwest Airlines 737 did a 2,175-foot belly slide instead of properly landing at New York's LaGuardia Airport. Six people were hospitalized, but nobody was seriously injured. The National Transportation Safety Board identified the problem as an "improper nose-down attitude" upon landing. This caused the forward gear to collapse, resulting in the frightening belly slide.

In flight, the *attitude* is the position of the nose of the airplane. While flying at a constant altitude (not going up or down), the body of the aircraft actually tilts slightly upward. The front end is higher than the back end. The same is true with us. Effective "cruising" requires us to always position our thoughts upward. If we focus too much on the world, we can start drifting towards it. Rough patches can result in anger, disappointment, bitterness, shame, or disillusionment. But these "nose-down" *attitudes* only serve to drive us in the wrong direction.

King David dealt with this. He failed God, his country, his family, and himself. But instead of getting "nose down," he turned his face upward, cried out to God, and allowed Him to adjust his attitude. From David's perspective, it wasn't an easy process. He suffered. His spirit was broken. But God corrected him, restored him, and enabled him to write many beautiful psalms that have inspired people for thousands of years.

> *"Bless the Lord, O my soul,*
> *And all that is within me, bless His holy name.*
> *Bless the Lord, O my soul,*
> *And forget none of His benefits;*
> *Who pardons all your iniquities,*
> *Who heals all your diseases;*
> *Who redeems your life from the pit,*
> *Who crowns you with lovingkindness and compassion;*
> *Who satisfies your years with good things,*
> *So that your youth is renewed like the eagle."*

Psalm 103:1–5

I like that he used the analogy of an eagle. If he were writing today, I'm sure he'd relate to the flight of airplanes! Note the upward tilt of David's spirit as he recounts the goodness of the Lord. Remembering "His benefits" fills us with the key component of a "nose-up" attitude, and that is gratitude.

As we come to comprehend the depth of God's unwarranted grace to save us and raise us up in new life, we cannot help but be deeply grateful. We were dead in our sin, but He brought us back to life. We were headed toward eternal separation from Him, but He promises eternal joy through Christ. We were on a path to destruction, but He put our feet on solid rock to give us peace, purpose, and power. If we cannot be grateful, we have forgotten His grace or disregarded His promises.

Suffering is difficult. Nobody's thankful for a debilitating or life-threatening disease. When loved ones are robbed, raped, or murdered, the natural reaction is certainly not gratefulness, nor should it be. Does God really expect us to maintain an attitude of gratefulness when sin has its way?

James wrote, *"Consider it all joy, my brethren, when you encounter various trials, knowing that the testing of your faith produces endurance"* (James 1:2–3). The gratefulness doesn't come as a result of the "various trials," but from the good work that God promises to bring as He carries us through bad circumstances. I don't believe for one second that we should ever develop a perverse joy for the pain that sin or the circumstances of this fallen world bring. Instead, we must remember the promises of God and the good things He guarantees to bring even through difficult times.

Paul Young, author of *The Shack* and *Cross Roads*, said something that rattled my thinking. A good friend of mine had lost his father to cancer and his mother to what should have been a routine operation within the span of two years. He descended into what he calls a "dark place." It was disconcerting to those of us around him, and no amount of encouragement seemed to penetrate his anger and despair. I handed him a copy of *The Shack*, hoping it would minister to him somehow. God used it in a remarkable way to begin walking him out of his darkness. A couple of years later, I was interviewing Paul about *Cross Roads*. After we finished, my friend came to the makeup room to thank Paul for *The Shack* and tell him how much it helped him. After hearing his story, Paul hugged my friend tightly and cried with him.

"The anger you feel about your parents' death is right," he said. This startled me. It didn't fit my "count it all joy" concept. He went on to point out that death wasn't God's original plan for mankind. Death is a result of the sin Adam and Eve brought into the world. Our anger with the pain it brings is akin to the hatred God has for sin. But if that was the end of it, we would have no cause for gratefulness. Paul encouraged my friend to find joy in the Hand that walked him through the darkness and brought him back into the light.

God's promise that He can work all things for good gives us hope. It's not that everything is good – it's not. It's the truth that He can take the wrongs of the world and make us right that gives us hope and makes us thankful. We do not celebrate disease, disaster, or other difficulties. Instead, we look forward to the good things God promises to bring as He carries us through every hardship. For this, we are then grateful.

The Roman philosopher Marcus Tullius Cicero wrote, "A thankful heart is not only the greatest virtue, but the parent of all the other virtues." Cultivating gratitude enables joy, kindness, peace, and other positive attitudes. It's an outlook that those around us will appreciate, but it benefits us personally most of all.

When we put our full faith in God, we can maintain this posture, even when things seem to be going down. By keeping our "nose up" and eyes focused above, we can maintain an attitude of gratefulness because we know the One who holds everything together and promises that we will ultimately land in His arms.

Angle of Attack

One way a pilot can increase the lift of an airplane is to increase the *angle of attack*. This is a somewhat relative term, because variables make different angles necessary. Wind direction and velocity, the type of airplane, and speed of the airplane require the pilot to have an understanding of the best position, but in all cases, the precise angle is critical to flight. An *angle of attack* that is too horizontal can result in diminished lift, while one that is too vertical can cause the aircraft to stall. To simplify it, the pilot must move beyond knowledge of his surroundings to develop wisdom in order to determine his proper *angle of attack*.

Life requires us to develop wisdom as well. Many situations don't allow for a one-size-fits-all mindset. There are variables that demand adjustments in our approach. We deal with our children differently than we deal with our co-workers. Even dealing with our children requires sensitivity to the situation. There will be times for discipline and firmness while other circumstances may require more tenderness and understanding. We must learn how to deal with these varying situations.

Wisdom is essentially "know how." Knowledge is the building block, but wisdom understands how to use that knowledge. Godly wisdom is the ability to choose Godly means for achieving a Godly outcome. As Christ-followers, we cannot settle for mere knowledge or human wisdom; we must pursue the wisdom from above, which is *"first pure, then peaceable, gentle, reasonable, full of mercy and good fruits, unwavering, without hypocrisy"* (James 3:17).

You can go to school, graduate with honors, earn multiple doctorates, and still be a fool in God's eyes. Our faith does not depend on *"the wisdom of men, but on the power of God* (1 Corinthians 2:5). Paul says that Christ Himself is God's wisdom.[1] God uses simple people of faith to shame those the world considers wise.[2]

Intelligent fools lack wisdom because they do not know how to properly apply their knowledge. As we come to know Christ better, we are able to learn how to apply His truth to our daily thoughts and activities. The scriptures promise us that *"if any of you lacks wisdom, let him ask of God, who gives to all generously and without reproach, and it will be given to him"* (James 1:5).

I like the story of the "wise men" at Christmas. These men, called magi, were astrologers. They searched the heavens for truth and understanding. But a few things separated them from the rest of the seers, interpreters, and soothsayers of their day, enabling us to call them "wise."

First, they recognized something significant in the heavens. We don't know how long they followed the stars, but it was apparently many months, because Herod, whom they visited before finding Jesus, later ordered all males around the age of two to be killed in an attempt to eliminate this child "king." (Herod was noted for his paranoia and rampant murder. Other historical accounts tell how he killed family members, including his wife and several sons.

....
[1] *1 Corinthians 1:24*
[2] *1 Corinthians 1:27*

On his deathbed, he ordered his men to kill Hebrews whom he knew would rejoice at his death so that mourning would be heard throughout the land instead.) Wise men recognize the presence of God, even in creation. *"The heavens are telling of the glory of God; And their expanse is declaring the work of His hands"* (Psalm 19:1).

It's amazing how people can gaze across our tiny portion of the universe, unlock pieces of our complex and intricately fashioned DNA, or study the millions of species on the land and in the oceans, yet maintain a certainty that there is no God. They should at least have the humility and intellectual honesty to be agnostic. Yet many foolishly and arrogantly claim that even though they know so little about the heavens and earth, they possess the knowledge that God does not exist. They are fools. They remain comfortable in their false sense of wisdom, which amounts to ignorant pride. But like the magi, wise men pursue knowledge and truth wherever it leads.

Second, the wise men searched diligently for Jesus. They weren't exactly sure what He looked like, but they knew they had to find Him. They journeyed far out of their way to discover God on earth. Wise men still do the same today. *"Draw near to God and He will draw near to you,"* James wrote (4:8). Jesus set out this principle too: *"Ask, and it will be given to you; seek, and you will find; knock, and it will be opened to you. For everyone who asks receives, and he who seeks finds, and to him who knocks it will be opened"* (Matthew 7:7–8).

One of my early favorite rock bands was the group *Live*. Though often angry and profane, their lyrics contained a spiritual depth that intrigued me. The lead singer, Ed Kowalczyk, maintained a website for a while called "Hole in the Universe." It was a brilliantly designed mishmash of religious imagery and eastern thought. Though raised in the Catholic church, Kowalczyk came to resent the religion of his youth and went on a spiritual exploration. Early albums reflect this with such songs as *Operation Spirit*, where he says Jesus "means nothing at all to me today."

Later albums, like *Secret Samadhi* (a reference to Buddhism's "Noble Eightfold Path"), included allusions to the Hindu goddess Lakini and the Indian guru Ramana Maharshi. But Kowalczyk didn't stop there; he kept searching. Now he has embraced Christianity and launched a solo career with songs such as *Grace* and *I'm The Proof*, which includes these lyrics:

"Won't you take a walk with me?
Down to the river
Where angels and sinners meet
Take a drink, I know you're thirsty

If you were, well I was too
Where you've gone, I've been there
I've chased that fire and got burned just like you

Sometimes people change
And I'm the proof."

Like the magi at Christ's birth, Ed Kowalczyk searched for wisdom and found it. You can too.

Third, the wise men fell to the ground and worshipped Him when they found Him. That was an act of great humility for such dignified men. It required true wisdom for grown men to recognize their inferiority to a child. The same is true today. When we come in humility and fall in worship, we demonstrate an awareness of who we are compared to who He is. We confess with our mouths and through our actions that we are in the presence of the one and only King. *"Every knee will bow,"* Romans 14:11 tells us. It takes a wise man to voluntarily bow down in worship.

Finally, they "opened their treasure" and gave gifts to Him. Gold, frankincense, and myrrh were not cheap offerings. They signified the best these men had. I can imagine people asking Mary and Joseph, "Where'd you get all this gold?" Their response: "Well, these magi showed up at our door one day and worshipped our child and gave us these valuable gifts." Talk about a baby shower!

When we give our very best to Christ, we demonstrate true wisdom. This doesn't just mean a tithe or even all of our possessions. It means the best of our talent, every moment of our day, our family, our passion – everything. Miraculously, we are not left destitute by giving all of it to Him. To the contrary, we find our needs met and our spirits overflowing with abundance. Giving our best really means exchanging a lesser treasure for the greater treasure of His provision and blessing. But it starts with giving.

The key to finding wisdom lies in the aggressive pursuit of it. It is not some unattainable ambition. God desires to give us His wisdom so that we instinctively know the best angle of attack in every situation.

Density Altitude

An airplane can successfully take off from a runway one day, but find it impossible to take off again the next. Why is that? Because of variations in the air from one day to the next, caused by several factors like temperature, humidity, and pressure. This *density altitude* is relative to atmospheric conditions and seasonal variations. Pilots use a wide array of gauges, charts, and reports to take these factors into account.

Life certainly has its seasonal variations for us. The spiritual atmosphere can change from one day to the next. Things can be fine today and seem to shift tomorrow. Knowing how to deal with these constantly changing circumstances requires discernment.

Discernment is the ability to know what is right in various situations. There are many absolutes that never change. A jet will never fly at 20 miles per hour. A crosswind will always try to push a plane off course. But there are many situations where the right answer is not always the same answer. The takeoff speed on a hot, muggy day in Miami is not the same as a clear, cool day in Denver. A discerning pilot will know the difference.

In our lives, we face varying circumstances. One stressful relationship may require confrontation while another may require patience and grace. Parents know that what works as effective discipline for one child may completely fail on another. Learning to deal with these variations requires Godly discernment.

This doesn't mean that there are no absolutes – there are. Sin always brings death. Jesus Christ always brings life. These things, and many others, don't change. Understanding absolute truth is actually the first step to developing true discernment. Paul says to *"examine everything carefully; hold fast to that which is good; abstain from every form of evil"* (1 Thessalonians 5:21–22). We must first know what is right and wrong in the context of what is of God and what is not. That means being firmly rooted in the Bible, understanding it, and properly applying truth to our individual circumstances.

It's like a pilot first learning the fundamentals of flying. If he doesn't know the proper takeoff speed of his aircraft, it doesn't matter whether he can discern between the nuances of ground elevation and air temperature. He has no understanding of the basic truths upon which to deal with the variations.

Learning the baseline of God's truth enables us to deal with the nuances. In the Old Testament, as God led the Israelites into the Promised Land, He dealt with the other tribes in several different ways. He told Moses to completely destroy the Canaanites, Amorites, and several others. None were to be spared.[3] For the sons of Anakim, God destroyed them Himself as a "consuming fire."[4] Later, He told them to first offer a peace treaty to cities. For those who refused, the Israelites were to kill the men, but spare the women, children, and animals.[5] Another time as Jehoshaphat led the armies of Judah, they didn't even fight. Instead, they sang songs of worship and their enemies killed each other.[6]

To the undiscerning mind, God might seem erratic, inconsistent, or arbitrary. But when we understand that there are certain baseline absolutes, like keeping the Lord's commandments,[7] standing strong, and fearing no man,[8] then these other things are merely seasonal variations. They simply require the ability to discern what is of God within the given context.

You and I will likely not be in the position to decide who to destroy and who to spare in times of war, but we will need to know when to stay at a job or leave, whether to donate to a worthy cause or put our finances elsewhere, how to approach people with needs or concerns, and what words to use when dealing with co-workers, neighbors, teachers, relatives, and friends. Every situation has its

....

[3] *Deuteronomy 7:1–2*
[4] *Deuteronomy 9:3*
[5] *Deuteronomy 20:13–14*
[6] *2 Chronicles 20:22–23*
[7] *Deuteronomy 8:6*
[8] *2 Chronicles 20:17*

nuances, and the way we interact with people requires a great deal of discernment. What flies in one relationship may wreck another.

There are baseline truths, like *"a kind answer turns away wrath"* (Proverbs 15:1) and *"be at peace with others as much as possible"* (Romans 12:18), but the specifics can vary. Some employees demand firmer treatment than others. Some children need more understanding and patience. Confronting a neighbor over an issue may cause them to be defensive and angry, or it may open them up to a deeper friendship. It's impossible for us to know how to handle every situation without the active direction of the Holy Spirit.

I believe that's why just before telling the church to examine everything carefully, Paul says to pray without ceasing.[9] Obviously this does not mean to eternally kneel or recite the Lord's Prayer. One would cause injury and the other would create pandemonium. It would not only be weird, but highly impractical. Certainly Paul didn't do that. What he means is to maintain open communication with the Holy Spirit in every circumstance. It means maintaining an awareness of His presence and an open ear to His voice at all times.

In fact, that very concept unlocks one of the secrets to developing discernment. Believers should not and must not go any place, do anything, or say any word that we cannot ask God's blessing upon. If you are trying to discern whether or not to watch a television show or movie, ask whether or not you can pray for God's blessing while you watch. If you want to know if it's alright to go to that party or vacation in that location, consider how comfortable you will be with the Holy Spirit by your side. You will find that there is not always a hard and fast rule about such things. Each situation must be led by God.

. . . .
[9] *1 Thessalonians 5:17*

That's why I have had to skip a friend's bachelor party, but I've been inside a brothel. The former was an environment I felt I should not put myself in, while the latter was an undercover video shoot in Southeast Asia. I can say with a clear conscience that both decisions were right because I discerned in each case that God was in my words and actions. In most cases, my friends have not had bachelor parties that were inappropriate, but the atmosphere was different on that one occasion. And brothel visits are certainly not normal for me. To date, that was the only time I've ever been in one, but again, the conditions were different. What wouldn't fly most days was part of my journey in that instance.

Without Godly discernment, navigating the seasonal variations of life is impossible. But the Holy Spirit stands ready to intervene in every situation. We just need to ask and listen. The more we learn this skill, the more effectively we can cruise successfully through each day.

Chapter 8 ....

FLIGHT PLAN

Every pilot needs to know how he's going to get from his departure to his destination. He needs a flight plan. When filed with the Federal Aviation Administration (FAA), the flight plan includes airport codes, cruising altitude, air speed, and other relevant information. Essentially, it's a checklist that proves the pilot has thoroughly considered and prepared for his flight ahead of time. It's also an insurance policy, in a sense, because if a pilot files a flight plan and does not arrive within half an hour of the scheduled time, the FAA will begin searching for the plane. When things go terribly wrong, a flight plan can potentially save lives.

Written Plan

Every pilot has an idea in his head as to what his journey will entail. But an actual flight plan puts it into writing. By spelling it out, it ensures the pilot has covered all the basic details. It also creates a record for others to use.

God gave us a flight plan. It's called *The Bible*. It's deep – really deep. You're not going to get bored with it. You can study it your whole life and still discover new things (not because it changes, but because your understanding continues to grow). At the same time, it's really not that difficult to dive into it and gain a lot of insight immediately.

The simplest way to start is to read the words of Christ in the Bible – the red letters in certain editions. These are the words God left us to attest of His Son. We could debate the veracity of the Bible and the methods used by the Council of Carthage to determine which books were included, but suffice to say that God is far more powerful than a group of men. I really can't imagine He's up in Heaven scratching His head saying, "I went through all that trouble to send my Son to save the world and those men screwed it up!" I do think an understanding of the original languages, mainly Hebrew and Greek, helps to clarify any misunderstandings that can come through translation, but the Holy Spirit is more than capable to enlighten us when we earnestly seek to know the truth. In fact, without the Holy Spirit's involvement in our spiritual growth, the Bible can easily become mere words on a page.

Scripture is a bit like a flight plan in that it applies to everyone, yet we each interface with it uniquely. In other words, the basics apply to everyone, yet we will each gain value from it at different points in our lives and for a variety of reasons. For the one struggling with depression, Psalm 42 will stand out. For the one battling doubt during difficult times, the first chapter of James will speak loudly. It's important to deal with each other graciously as we execute different parts of our flight plan. We're not all on the exact same journey. Someone who's flying lower or slower than you should be encouraged in their efforts, not belittled as inferior.

A German theologian of the early 17th century named Rupertus Meldenius said, "In essentials unity; in non-essentials liberty; in all things charity." The words of Christ are essentials. The overall theme of Scripture is essential. Religious preferences, styles, and other variations that do not contradict the essentials are non-essential. In flight, a minimum air speed is essential. Anything slower will result in a stall and a fall; but between the minimum and the maximum, there is an acceptable range. In our faith, there is also an acceptable range, allowing for variety and expression. It's important that we understand what falls within that range and allow others to travel at their appropriate speed.

I grew up singing out of hymnals, but I'm happy to never see one again. It's just not my style. There's nothing holy or righteous in using or not using one. That's the beauty of God's creation. We are all different and each relate, within bounds of Scripture, to God in our own way. Some prefer the quiet solitude of a cathedral while others prefer the noisy jubilee of a tent revival. Those things are non-essential, and we should treat the preferences of others with charity, while maintaining the essential core of the simple and direct Gospel of Jesus Christ. We should allow for the various expressions of worship under the banner of Paul's greeting in Galatians:

"Grace to you and peace from God our Father and the Lord Jesus Christ, who gave Himself for our sins so that He might rescue us from this present evil age, according to the will of our God and Father, to whom be the glory forevermore."
Galatians 1:3–5

All believers are here to glorify our God the Father. We strive to understand and apply the words of Christ in our lives. In this, we are one. How we best do that will look a little different, and that's perfectly acceptable. Some may draw closer to God primarily through meditation and prayer, others through intense study of Scripture. Some may sit in silence while others celebrate in noisy praise. God loves it all. As we seek to know and proclaim God's simple truths, we must maintain a balance of grace toward others.

Simultaneously, that balance demands we adhere to the essentials of our written plan. Pilots must contend with five different classifications of controlled airspace dealing with issues such as airport proximity and radio communication capabilities. They must be apprised of temporary flight restrictions, like special rules around air shows and natural hazards such as wildfires. They have to know about restricted areas like those where military exercises are underway. And they must always avoid prohibited areas like the space around the White House. These are essentials designed to help a pilot avoid danger.

The Bible is full of essentials, many designed to help us avoid danger. Much of the Old Testament law is akin to temporary flight restrictions – special rules for a time to keep the Israelites from harm. Things like dietary restrictions, Sabbath guidelines, and instructions for approaching the altar were, in essence, temporary regulations for their time. Other things are highly restricted, such as rules regarding divorce and requirements for those in church leadership. Some things are absolutely prohibited, like sexual immorality.

Knowing how to read God's flight plan helps provide insurance against our own harm. It is both restrictive and liberating, because once we learn how to avoid harm, we are free to fly more securely, providing for a safer, smoother journey. He has already filed it; we simply need to read it, understand it, and allow it to guide our journey.

Course Corrections

One element of the FAA's flight plan is the route of flight. This is separate from the origination and destination. It provides a pathway, whether a direct route or one with necessary adjustments, like flying around a mountain or restricted airspace. Conforming to this route is critical to the wellbeing of the passengers and crew. If an airplane strays, there are safety measures to help get it back on course.

In Romans, Paul points out an important part of keeping us on course:

> *"And do not be conformed to this world, but be transformed by the renewing of your mind, so that you may prove what the will of God is, that which is good and acceptable and perfect."*
> Romans 12:2

When we break down the Greek connotation of this passage, we get a better idea of exactly what it means. Being "conformed" means to pattern your mind and character after the world. Nonconformity doesn't mean you drive a different car or listen to unpopular music. It means you don't think and act like unbelievers.

Transformation is the converse of conformity. It means to change into another form. It parallels Christ's transfiguration, where He became radiant in front of His disciples and Moses and Elijah appeared with Him. The significance lies in the connection between the earthly and the heavenly, the human and the divine.

Paul is suggesting that our minds must become divinely changed on a daily basis. This is done by "renewing," which is defined as a "complete change for the better."

Another connotation of the word is "renovation." When you renovate your home or office, you get rid of the old stuff and bring in new furnishings, flooring, fixtures, and décor. A newly renovated room looks different because it has been updated and reorganized. Transforming our minds gets rid of the old thoughts and patterns and upgrades them with a divine arrangement. It puts us on the right course for a successful journey.

The mind includes the intellect, feelings, judgment, and reasoning. It is with your mind that you recognize the difference between right and wrong, good and evil, what is of God and what is not. It includes your desires and your purpose for doing and saying things. It is the mechanism by which you become able to perceive the things of God.

When your mind is transformed to God's patterns and your thoughts and perceptions change, you are able to "prove" the will of God. By this, Paul doesn't mean that we win some kind of theological argument. The word "prove" has a chemistry connection, in the same way that metals are tested to validate their authenticity. Proving the will of God in our lives means examining an idea to know whether it is genuinely His. It's developing the skill of discernment to validate and implement His will in the same way precious metals are examined to prove their authenticity.

The will of God aligns with His commandments in Scripture, His principles, His desires, and His pleasure. It comprises the choices we make every single day. Do our thoughts, words, and actions align with His will? Transforming these things from their natural, destructive course into His superior, life-giving ways achieves His will in our lives.

This daily exercise of rejecting ungodly patterns and ideas by aligning our thoughts, emotions, and desires with God's nature and Word gives us the ability to make Godly choices and develop righteous habits. Failing to do this throws us off course, even if only slightly. If an airplane is just barely off course, that issue compounds with time. An inch becomes a foot, which becomes a yard, which becomes a mile. The longer the pilot maintains his improper course, the further off he gets. Without course corrections, that pilot will find himself a long way from his intended destination.

Before Global Positioning Systems (GPS), airplanes verified their positions with the help of marker beacons. These fixed-point radio transmitters kept pilots on the right track to help them arrive safely. We have several spiritual marker beacons to help us properly navigate our faith. These are the "fruit of the Spirit."

If you want a checklist to see if you're on course, look no further than Galatians 5:22–23:

"But the fruit of the Spirit is love, joy, peace, patience, kindness, goodness, faithfulness, gentleness, self-control; against such things there is no law."

When you're cruising on course, these things will automatically light up, like beacons in the night. You won't have to show them off; they will inherently illuminate the darkness of this world. They will testify to the fact that you are set on a supernaturally powered path.

When we look at the biblical analogy of fruit, we notice that trees don't strive to produce them. When watered and left undisturbed, a tree will routinely produce fruit. Apple trees will make apples. Orange trees will produce oranges. People will see it, partake of it, and benefit from it.

The same is true with you. As you live more each day under the Holy Spirit's guidance and think, speak, and act more like Christ, these things will occur. By His grace He has set this principle in motion. It moves us in powerful ways that lift our faith. We seek the refreshing water of His Word, bask in the warmth of His Spirit, and witness the growth of beautiful, life-giving fruit.

It's interesting that Paul notes that *"against such things there is no law"* (Galatians 5:23). When we consider the law as a weight, we can see how the weightlessness of love, joy, peace, patience, kindness, goodness, faithfulness, gentleness, and self-control naturally lift us. They are not only markers to confirm our course, but an uplifting breeze upon which we can effortlessly glide further and higher. When this happens, others will see it. When they experience it for themselves, it will provide them with spiritual *lift* and point them toward Heaven.

None of us will cruise through life without needing a course correction. Jesus didn't come into this world to condemn us, but to guide us. We must have the humility to change direction when we realize that we are off course.

Veracity

Douglas "Wrong-Way" Corrigan holds an unusual and amusing place in American history. A former mechanic for Charles Lindbergh, the Texas native gained national attention by flying from California to New York in what was considered to be a "rattletrap." Upon arrival in New York, he quickly sought to match Lindbergh's transatlantic feat by flying his rebuilt 1929 Curtiss Robin aircraft from Newfoundland to Ireland. He filed a flight plan and was immediately denied permission. His airplane was simply too old and unreliable.

So on July 17, 1938, Corrigan took off from Floyd Bennett Field in New York City to return to California. At least, that's what his new flight plan said. Instead, the aviator flew across the Atlantic and, 28 hours later, arrived in Dublin, Ireland. Upon landing, he reportedly said, "Just got in from New York. Where am I?"

Authorities were not amused. They suspended his license despite his story that he got lost in the clouds when his compass malfunctioned. But by the time Corrigan returned from Ireland to the United States on a steamer, his story had grabbed the attention of a Depression-racked public, and they hailed him as a hero. When he disembarked in New York City, he was a greeted by an enthusiastic crowd. The next day, the mayor gave him a ticker-tape parade down Broadway. President Franklin Roosevelt claimed he never doubted Corrigan's story, and the famous pilot stuck by it to the end. RKO Studios even made a movie about him called *The Flying Irishman*.

Corrigan's story is colorful and entertaining, but filing false documents or straying from a flight plan is a serious crime. More recently, falsified documents have been tied to the crashes that killed the hugely-popular Hispanic singer, Jenni Rivera, and the Russian airline that decimated the Lokomotiv Yaroslavl hockey team, killing many former NHL players, including the remarkable Kārlis Skrastiņš. When it comes to modern flight, truthfulness in the flight plan and related documents is critical.

The fact that lying cannot be a habit of those who follow the One who *is* truth should be fairly obvious. If that's your pattern, you need to repent (change your mind about it) and forsake such deception immediately. Most believers don't fall into such an obvious trap, which is why I believe the enemy tempts us with several more subtle forms of untruthfulness.

The first of these is self-deception. Perhaps the easiest person to routinely lie to is yourself. This hides in a wide range of disguises. We convince ourselves that we cannot be used by God because we are not worthy. We act as if God can forgive anything except what we've done. We tell ourselves that our hidden thoughts won't ever hurt anyone, even though they're killing us. We promise to deal with issues tomorrow and never do. Anything in our thoughts, actions, and attitudes that doesn't line up with Truth, which is Jesus Christ, is *un*truth. The only way to realign our lives is to agree with God and act on it. We must start believing what He says about us and resist every impulse to hide, justify, procrastinate, ignore, or otherwise bury our imperfections. Yes, God loves us even in our sin, but He doesn't want us to live there!

Self-deception is a prison that we build, often to create a false sense of security. But instead of protecting us, it ultimately keeps us locked in a state of uselessness. You'll never see prisoners carrying out the Great Commission. The key to escaping this trap is complete honesty about ourselves and a daily encounter with Truth Himself. This false view must be wiped clean by looking into the mirror of God's Word and seeing ourselves as Christ does.

Another slippery slope into untruthfulness lies in what journalists like to call *spin*. Decorated journalist and Nixon speechwriter William Safire defines *spin* in political journalism as "deliberate shading of news perception; attempted control of political reaction."[1] In everyday life, we can describe spin as purposely distorting the truth to make ourselves look or feel better.

....

[1] *"New Political Dictionary" by William Safire (Random House).*

Take, for example, the man who compares his marriage to everyone else's. Given the high rate of divorce and even higher rate of rotten relationships, it's easy to think, "Mine is better than most." But we are not called to a standard of better-than-average. We are called to a marital relationship that Christ used as an analogy of His relationship to His people. He calls the church His bride.

> "Husbands, love your wives, just as Christ also loved the church and gave Himself up for her."
>
> Ephesians 5:25

That's what God desires in our relationships. Settling for less is an untruthful proposition, even if it looks good related to everyone else.

Other forms of *spin* easily found among believers are really manipulation. Exaggeration is an almost accepted form of deceit, frivolously called "evangelistically speaking." C.S. Lewis smartly said, "Don't use words too big for the subject. Don't say infinitely when you mean very; otherwise you'll have no word left when you want to talk about something really infinite."[2] Habitual hyperbole eventually wears off, resulting in a reverse of the intended effect. Those who catch on to the exaggeration become unimpressed by anything the speaker says, even the things genuinely impressive. A pastor once told me that a story worth repeating is worth embellishing. He smiled as he said this, but his joke is rooted in reality. This practice is typically untruthfulness for the sake of manipulating an audience.

....
[2] *C. S. Lewis' Letters to Children*

Flattery for the sake of controlling others also forsakes truth. Proverbs 29:5 says, *"A man who flatters his neighbor is spreading a net for his steps."* This is not the same as legitimately complimenting someone or speaking words of encouragement. The Hebrew idea for flattery includes division, apportion, and plunder. When we use words of praise in order to win someone to our side or get something from him or her, it becomes an act of selfishness. We should avoid ever doing this, and steer clear of those who do.

Using Scripture for our own gain, typically in fragments and often out of context, also fails the truth test. God's Word is designed to draw us to Him, not to a certain church or person. His Word is a lamp for our feet and light to our path,[3] not another man's bit in our mouth or whip on our back. When a person uses the Bible to bring us under his or her power, this is an evil, cult-like invocation of Scripture. Again, we must avoid ever doing this and run from those who attempt to control us in this manner.

All forms of untruthfulness must be purged from our lips and from our lives. It is truly the "wrong way." A false flight plan will not make you a hero. Only when we fully embrace God's truth can we honestly share His truth with others.

....
[3] *Psalm 119:105*

Chapter 9

DANGERS

Flying has inherent risks. Mechanical issues can cause failure. The atmosphere can be hostile. Evil people can hurt innocent people. We all know and accept these risks when we board a flight, but the smart traveler pays attention. If something's amiss, he or she reports it to the flight crew. An alert ground crew detects a defect on the outside of the plane. A diligent pilot runs through his checklist and catches any signal that something might be wrong. A sharp flight attendant notices a passenger behaving curiously. We don't know how many disasters have been averted by people simply being aware of dangerous situations and taking steps to prevent them, but there is no doubt that attentiveness has paid off many times and countless lives have been saved.

Paul talked about Satan's schemes, not wanting believers to be unaware of them. We must not lull ourselves into a false sense of security by ignoring the fact that dangers do exist, and not all of them are merely incidental. Some are purposeful plans of our enemy. We must be alert and diligent to avoid falling prey.

Turbulence

There is not much on this earth that rattles me more than turbulence on a flight. Every chop and bump drives my prayer life up a notch. I have been known to pray out loud on particularly rough flights. Even the anticipation of it causes ridiculous anxiety. But turbulence is a part of flying. It's going to happen. Learning to deal with it, and the fear it can cause, is critical to staying on course.

Pilots know how to deal with turbulence. They will go over or around a developing thunderstorm. They may increase or decrease airspeed to better ride out unavoidable bumps. Even the design of an airplane takes turbulence into account as the wings flex to make the ride smoother. Still, it happens. Knowing the causes helps pilots avoid it, but they still must know how to deal with it when it does occur.

Most turbulence is the result of change. Variations in wind speed or direction and fluctuations in temperature create instability, which results in chop, bumps, and full-blown turbulence. Though the instances are low, injuries and deaths do occur, usually because the person is not buckled up. I was waiting to use the restroom while flying from Hong Kong to Los Angeles when things got rough over the Sea of Japan really fast. As I struggled to get back to my seat, the flight attendants were already seated and strapped in. They were speaking Chinese to me, but their urgent message was clear: Sit down and buckle up!

Life is full of changes. Many can be predicted, but the ones that cause the most trouble are those for which we are not prepared. One way to prepare is to be flexible. Like the design of the wings, we must construct ourselves emotionally and spiritually in a way that doesn't snap when we hit a rough patch. Inflexibility on our part makes the jolts even more jarring. Fixating on a philosophy or even a theology can be risky because if we are wrong, we can break. Maintaining a teachable spirit allows us to grow in Him even through difficult circumstances. Trusting that the Lord will guide us through the changes allows us to bend without breaking. This requires us to truly depend on Him, not our own perception and understanding of things.

The roughest flight I've ever experienced actually occurred without a cloud in the sky. It was so bad that the girl sitting next to me was crying. Others were moaning out loud. However, I was much more spiritual. I was quoting Matthew 8:25, *"Save us, Lord; we are perishing!"* Judging by the sudden announcement and vague prediction as to its length, the turbulences caught the pilots off guard too.

This phenomenon, known as *clear-air turbulence*, often surprises pilots and passengers because there is no warning that a rough ride is in store. Even when things seem to be going smoothly, unforeseen bumps can occur. *Clear-air turbulence* is in many ways more unnerving than being in a storm. At least with a storm, you know you're in for some action. When everything appears to be calm, but it's not, the inexplicability of it all creates real anxiety. The solution, both in the skies and in our lives, is to be prepared at all times. Learning to trust God through the changes provides a safety belt for every ride.

Full-fledged storms are not only rough, but dangerous. Visibility becomes a problem and winds can threaten to flip the plane upside down. Pilots have to rely on their instruments to guide them so they don't stall or become inverted. Our stormiest times of life can make it hard to see past our immediate circumstances. If we rely on our own sight instead of allowing the Holy Spirit to be our compass, our thoughts and feelings can get inverted. In every turbulent and stormy season, we must stay "buckled up" in Christ and focused on His direction.

Paul provided simple and direct guidance as he encouraged the church in Corinth: *"Be on the alert, stand firm in the faith, act like men, be strong"* (1 Corinthians 16:13). When we break down the original language of that verse, we see several key exhortations.

First, we must be alert, which means "to take heed lest through remission and indolence some destructive calamity suddenly overtake one."[1] That means proactively being prepared. Sometimes a situation creates more problems than necessary because our guard is down. We're metaphorically asleep. Spiritual laziness – neglecting to pray, study the Word, and put our faith into practice – allows unexpected changes to toss us around emotionally. Discipline in our daily walk is not just a way to please the Lord; it's a way to protect ourselves from the difficulties of life.

Second, we are to stand firm in the faith. That means holding on to our conviction of the truth of Jesus Christ – His teachings and promises. In the Epistle of James, he warns against wavering in faith because *"the one who doubts is like the surf of the sea, driven and tossed by the wind"* (James 1:6). We will be "in the wind" in the sense that difficulties will come. That much is guaranteed. Conviction is the seat belt that keeps us from being "driven and tossed" when turbulent times arise. If the loss of a job, for example, causes one to doubt God's provision, then worry and panic will likely set in. But if we hold fast to the truth that God will take care of us, we can maintain a sense of peace throughout the changing conditions. Standing firm in the faith is not a posture designed to

----

[1] *Thayer and Smith. "Greek Lexicon entry for Gregoreuo".*
"The NAS New Testament Greek Lexicon". 1999.

prove that we are somehow worthy of God's blessings, but more a means of protecting ourselves from the destruction that a lack of resolve can bring.

Third, we must "act like men." There are a dozen jokes that could be written about that line, but the Greek word used there has more to do with attitude than gender. It simply means to be brave. To be honest, I could fly into a hurricane if I knew with absolute certainty that we would safely fly out of it. My anxiety is not actually caused by bouncing around in the air, but by the underlying concern that the plane won't make it safely to its destination. Turbulence just exacerbates that fear. If we fear that God's promises are not true, like perhaps He doesn't really love us or maybe He really is out to punish us rather than redeem us, then the jolts of life will intensify those ideas and wreak havoc. When we know that He will never abandon us, will work all things together for good for those who love Him, and will receive us into His presence for eternity, then we can bravely fly through any storm with absolute certainty that we will make it to the other side safely.

Finally, we must "be strong," which is really better interpreted as "grow strong." The implication of the original phrase is that as we go through difficulties, we are not weakened by them, but rather increased in our strength. The Bible is full of people who faced difficult, if not impossible, situations and became stronger because of it. Moses faced Pharaoh. Joshua faced the Canaanites and other hostile tribes. David faced Goliath. Esther faced King Xerxes. Shadrach, Meshach, and Abednego faced Nebuchadnezzar. Daniel faced the lions. Simon Peter would have faced King Herod, but an angel miraculously sprung him from prison. Jesus, of course, faced the Jewish and Roman leaders and death itself. All of them grew stronger because they didn't back down in the midst of adversity.

As we face our various trials, we must remember their lives and heed Paul's advice to stay strong.

In this life, turbulence will happen. Storms hit us all – the righteous and unrighteous alike.[2] We inhabit imperfect bodies in a fallen world. Believing we will somehow never be shaken denies the very words of Christ. *"In the world you have tribulation,'"* He told His followers. Fortunately, He didn't stop there. *"But take courage; I have overcome the world'"* (John 16:33).

It's interesting that He didn't say, "The world could cause problems, but don't worry about it because I'll keep you away from them." He definitely asserted His authority over every problem we face, but He still said we would face them. He didn't come to rescue us from turbulence, but to ride it out with us. Even when we are badly shaken, He's still there. Given His eternal perspective, He overcomes everything eventually – even death. Buckling up in His truth and holding on to His promises will give us the strength to face whatever may come.

Crashes

Statistically, about half of all crashes are due to pilot error. Another 20–25 percent of crashes result from mechanical failure. Manufacturers, airlines, the FAA, and other aeronautical organizations spend a great deal of time and money working to eliminate these issues. As a result, air travel is the safest form of travel today.

In the church, most spiritual disasters are due to human error. Some might be traced back to systemic problems within a church organization (a sort of religious mechanical failure), but ultimately it comes down to problems in individual thinking and judgment.

....
[2] *Matthew 5:45*

The major condition among believers leading to spectacular falls is what Jesus called "hardness of heart." Andrew Wommack calls it "the equivalent of spiritual retardation."[3] Like an airplane that takes off on ice and becomes unmanageable, knowing the truth but not acting on it freezes up our ability to think and behave correctly.

A pastoral friend of mine was caught in an affair with his children's nanny. Later, after he confessed, repented, and accepted every restorative measure placed on him, he told me, "I feel like such an idiot." I could only agree with him and encourage him to continue the right path he was on. He knew better – and he *knew* that he knew better – but had become blind to the truth that was right in front of him. So he chose, for a time, to believe that he could find satisfaction in the wrong place. His heart had become dull to the very Gospel he was eloquently preaching every weekend.

If you're thinking, *I would never do anything that bad*, be careful. Hardening your heart is easier than you may imagine, especially since it's something you don't do on purpose. It usually comes with time, like a pilot that flies so much that he becomes too comfortable and gets sloppy.

The concept of "hardness of heart" comes from an account of Jesus and His disciples. The setting was in the countryside near the Sea of Galilee. Jesus taught a large group of people for three days straight. It was like a massive tent revival without the tent. People came from all around, some from a "great distance." Mark puts the total number of people at about 4,000, which likely includes families and servants of those who were listening to Christ's teachings.

On the third day, food started running out. Jesus noticed. He saw their need. He discussed it with His disciples, who commented

....
[3] http://www.awmi.net/extra/article/hardness_heart

that food would be difficult to find in their "desolate place." They searched for food and came up with seven loaves of bread – clearly not enough. So there they were out in the middle of nowhere with not hundreds, but *thousands* of hungry people and only seven loaves of bread. They scrounged up a few small fish too, and sat the people down to eat. Sounds crazy, doesn't it?

Remember the Carnival cruise ship that had a fire in the engine room way out in the Gulf of Mexico and took several days to be towed back to port? About 4,000 passengers had no power, no running water, and no air-conditioning for several days. People made tents on the deck and dragged mattresses outside to sleep in the open air. Now imagine that they had run out of food and you were in charge of greeting them when they finally made it to port in Mobile, Alabama. You gather all of them in a warehouse and say, "Okay, we've got seven hamburgers and a few fish-sticks. Eat up!" Not a promising scenario.

But when Jesus told His disciples to prepare these people for a meal, they did as He asked. They had seen this before. Mark 6 records the same type of incident with an even larger crowd. After everyone was served – *everyone* – there were "seven large baskets" of scraps left over.

Once the crowd's need was satisfied, Jesus and the 12 got in a boat and sailed to a region called Dalmanutha. There, the local religious leaders came to Jesus and asked Him to perform a miraculous sign from Heaven. Jesus responded by basically saying, "These guys just want a sign, so I'm not giving it to them." Instead, they got back on the boat and left. (It's interesting to note that Jesus will do whatever it takes to care for those who believe in Him, but He's reluctant to perform for those who don't believe in Him.)

Back out on the water, Jesus started talking about the Pharisees they had just left. He used an analogy of rotten food to point out that just a little rottenness spoils the whole dish. And just like typical men, all the disciples heard was a story about food, which prompted them to say, "Hey, we don't have any food!"

Suddenly, food became the hot topic, not the message Jesus was trying to get through to them. I suspect this irritated Christ a bit, because He said to them, *"Why do you discuss the fact that you have no bread? Do you not yet see or understand? Do you have a hardened heart?"* (Mark 8:17).

The disciples knew that Jesus had always taken care of them. They knew He could miraculously feed thousands, much less a dozen. Still, they thought they had a problem.

"Having eyes, do you not see?" Jesus asked. *"And having ears, do you not hear?"* He even reminded them of the miracles they had seen. *"And do you not remember, when I broke the five loaves for the five thousand, how many baskets full of broken pieces you picked up?"* They answered, *"Twelve."* Jesus pressed them further. *"When I broke the seven for the four thousand, how many large baskets full of broken pieces did you pick up? They answered, "Seven."* Still, they didn't get it. *"Do you not yet understand?"* He asked (Mark 8:17–21, paraphrased).

The disciples heard Christ's teachings. They had seen Him at work. But they weren't acting like it in the boat that day. We can be this way: thick-headed, deaf, and blind to the truth – even when it's right in front of us. Hardness of heart is trying to fulfill our own needs by our own means when Christ has proven He is the only one who can truly fulfill them.

This is usually the underlying problem when we fall into disastrous sin. The Christian husband who cheats on his wife *knows* that he's making a mistake. He fully understands that his error could destroy his family and reputation. He even admits that God sees it. Yet he does it anyway. Why? Because his heart is hard. The truth is right in front of him, but he has forgotten that only Christ can fulfill his real needs.

It's the same for the person who commits fraud or theft because of financial pressure. He or she can only see that there's no food in the boat, despite the fact that Christ has repeatedly and miraculously provided for His followers.

It's even the same for the ones who sit in church hearing the pastor preach truth from the Bible, but only think about their problems when the service ends. Just as the hungry disciples couldn't hear the lesson Christ was teaching, we can easily focus on our physical and emotional desires when God is speaking directly to our spiritual needs. Any time we look anywhere but Christ to provide for us, we harden our hearts. This human error positions us for a crash. If we don't correct it, we will eventually hit the ground hard.

When we hear the words of Christ and see Him at work in our lives, but stop acting like it, we are no longer aligned with our professed beliefs, and our hearts become a little harder. We must take action to do as instructed by His Word and the Holy Spirit. Failing to do so results in "pilot error." But hearing and heeding enables us to correct our course by realigning our thoughts and actions to His truth. Staying alert to this danger and purposely honing sensitivity to His guidance helps us avoid painful personal disasters.

Terrorism

September 11, 2001 is a date that every American and most others around the world remember. On that day, millions watched on television as airplanes were hijacked by Islamists and flown into the World Trade Center and the Pentagon. Another went down in rural Pennsylvania after passengers tried to regain control of the plane. It was a shocking reminder that evil exists in the world and that malevolent forces seek our destruction.

It would be easy to focus merely on the people who carry out such wicked schemes, but the truth goes beyond mortal men. Satan is the ultimate terrorist. His mission is to steal, kill, and destroy people.[4] When he rose up against God and was cast out of Heaven, he took one-third of the angels with him.[5] Scripture treats these spiritual forces as real, living beings actively at work on this earth. Jesus spoke to them directly, not as metaphors but as individual spirits tormenting people. At the same time, He publicly displayed His authority over them.

In one instance, a man was harassed by a whole faction of demonic spirits. Jesus not only spoke to them, but conversed with them. In the end, He demonstrated His power to free the man of these tormentors and allowed them to enter a herd of swine. The animals promptly hurled themselves over a cliff and into the sea.[6] Several critically important truths are illustrated here.

First, demonic spirits are the filthiest of the filthy. Though it's not explicitly stated, I believe Jesus allowed the legion of demons to enter the swine to show how nasty the spirits were. Swine were considered unclean under Judaic law, and when the demons entered them, these filthy beasts couldn't even tolerate the foul spirits' level of filth. If unclean animals were repulsed by the demons, how much

---

[4] John 10:10
[5] Revelation 12:4
[6] Mark 5:1–20

more should we be? There is only one thing to be done with any spirit that is not of God: throw it away.

Second, the mission of Satan and his minions is nothing but torment. It's not politically-correct, feel-good tolerance to back down from or bow down to evil spirits. Granted, the Holy Spirit does not force Himself on anyone. He offers us the choice, sometimes boldly like He did to Saul on the road to Damascus, but never against our wishes. We can choose the company of demons, but doing so invites ruin. We should warn others accordingly. People that spurn the Holy Spirit and embrace the legions of hell cannot blame God when, like the swine, they are plunged into the depths of destruction. But like Christ, we must be ready to rescue people from the torment of the evil one and redeem them for eternal peace, joy, and glory.

Third, every evil power flees in the presence of Jesus Christ. They literally freak out. Satan's horde is terrified of Almighty God and cowers when He is near. Contrary to Hollywood's depiction of exorcisms, hauntings, and other supernatural activities, demons don't throw God's people around the room, vomit pea soup on them, or make their eyes pop out of their heads. When the Holy Spirit arrives, demons turn and run. They may roar like lions, but when faced with the power of Christ, they scatter like roaches. We never need to fear them. They only have such power as we allow by not abiding in Him. Defeating them is as simple as inviting the Holy Spirit into our lives. In a dogfight with God, demons are paper airplanes dueling with an F-22 Raptor. When He moves, even His exhaust burns them up.

Now that we have evil spirits in their proper perspective, how else should we prepare to deal with them?

First, like prospective terrorists in an airport, we must be vigilant against them. *"Put on the full armor of God,"* Paul wrote in his classic passage on spiritual warfare, *"so that you will be able to stand firm against the schemes of the devil"* (Ephesians 6:11). He goes on to describe the spiritual weapons and defenses given to us, including the helmet of salvation to guard our minds, the shield of faith to extinguish the flaming darts of the enemy, and the sword of the Spirit, an offensive weapon, which is the Word of God. We have what we need to win; we simply must be ready to engage in the fight.

Second, we must know spiritual terrorism when we see it. Controversy continues to surround the Transportation Security Administration at airports. When they screen too many Arabs, charges of racial profiling abound. When they screen too many elderly women instead of young men, charges of idiotic political correctness abound. When they miss something, charges of incompetency abound. Spiritually, we have to be better than the TSA. We have to learn to discriminate properly. Paul says that even Satan himself masquerades as an angel of light.[7] If we don't know the difference between the devil and a messenger of God, we are in worse shape than a blind man behind the x-ray machine at airport security (which is a great idea for a hidden-camera prank show).

One big clue as to the spirit behind something is whether it brings life and peace versus hostility and death. Paul wrote, *"For the mind set on the flesh is death, but the mind set on the Spirit is life and peace, because the mind set on the flesh is hostile toward God . . . "* (Romans 8:6–7a). Things that feed the desires of the human flesh should set off your spiritual metal detector. Spirits

....
[7] *2 Corinthians 11:14*

setting themselves in opposition to God by feeding our flesh are up to no good. We must learn to spot them, apprehend them, and throw them out before they can do any damage.

Third, we are not demon hunters. Our mission is to share His light, which automatically drives out the darkness. We must avoid focusing on the thrill of supernatural supremacy. The seven sons of Sceva in the book of Acts wanted to cast out demons, but they were stripped and beaten because they were not led by the Holy Spirit.[8] Jesus was aware of this tendency to be fascinated by demonic activity. After sending out 70 of His disciples to expand God's Kingdom on earth, the Gospels record the results:

> *"The seventy returned with joy, saying, 'Lord, even the demons are subject to us in Your name.' And He said to them, 'I was watching Satan fall from heaven like lightning. Behold, I have given you authority to tread on serpents and scorpions, and over all the power of the enemy, and nothing will injure you. Nevertheless do not rejoice in this, that the spirits are subject to you, but rejoice that your names are recorded in heaven.'"*
> Luke 10:17–20

Keeping our focus on the good is important. Otherwise, we'll start finding a demon in every nook, cranny, and overhead compartment. They are not to be feared or followed. Like terrorists, we must watch for them, know how to deal with them, and face them boldly. At the same time, we don't live our lives bound by the threat of them. We don't avoid dealing with them, but we don't toy with them. We boot them out of the way and get on with God's business.

....
[8] *Acts 19:11–16*

PREVENTION

If I was in an airplane crash, I would prefer to survive. But I'd rather not be in a crash! A little prevention certainly goes a long way when it comes to flying. The same is true in our lives. Too many people are destroyed by something that could easily have been prevented. One way to do so, at least in theory, would be to spend every moment trying not to make a big mistake. Many religious people seem to live this way. To me, that sounds like a miserable way to exist. It would be like grounding an airplane to ensure it never crashes.

I would propose that the best way to prevent a personal disaster is to do what airlines do: train their personnel, maintain their equipment, and perform routine inspections of both people and planes. We can train ourselves in the ways of God, maintain the growth we have achieved, and be held accountable through relationships with other believers.

Training

According to the FAA's Introduction to Flight Training manual, the purpose of training is "the acquisition and honing of basic airmanship skills." Airmanship is then defined in three ways: a sound acquaintance with the principles of flight, the ability to operate an airplane with competence and precision, and the exercise of sound judgment.

Biblical training could be defined similarly. It helps us grasp the principles of Christianity, enables us to live with spiritual competence, and gives us the basis for sound judgment in our daily decisions. Much of what Christ did on this earth was essentially training. We call it "discipleship."

The word "disciple" implies discipline. This is the training part of our faith. When Christ trained the 12 apostles, as well as the larger group of disciples, he taught them what they needed to know to spread the Kingdom of God here on earth. Before they went out, they went through training.

Too often, we want to go out and spread our wings without being properly trained in Christ. We have not acquired and honed the basic skills necessary, and we end up like the student pilot who contacted the control tower and said, "I'm lost. I'm over a big lake and heading toward the big E." The controller looked for small planes heading east, but couldn't spot him. "Make several 90-degree turns so I can identify you on radar," he replied. The novice aviator complied and a few minutes later, the control tower operated responded, "That big lake is the Atlantic Ocean. Turn to the big w immediately!"

Jesus spent time with His disciples. He walked with them, ate with them, and taught them many things. Those closest to Him left everything behind to spend a few short years under His tutelage.

The time was relatively short for them, but when He left, He made a provision for them, which extends to us today. *"I will ask the Father, and He will give you another Helper, that He may be with you forever . . . "* (John 14:16).

He was talking about the Holy Spirit, who is with us forever. He is our control tower – our guide when we can't find our way. It's easy to take off with just enough knowledge to get us into trouble. Without the Holy Spirit, we tend to go east when we need to go west. But if we will listen, He will tell us when to make the right turn to get back on course. He will train us, make us competent, and give us sound judgment. We just need to listen.

The goal of one in training is to graduate. Granted, we will never be complete until we reach Heaven, but there should come a time when we grasp the basics and begin to teach others. The apostles were far from complete when Jesus was crucified and rose from the grave, but before He ascended into Heaven, He gave this instruction:

> *"'Go therefore go and make disciples of all nations, baptizing them in the name of the Father and of the Son and of the Holy Spirit, and teaching them to obey everything I have commanded you. And surely I am with you always, to the very end of the age.'"*
>
> Matthew 28:18–20

We learn, then we teach. We are disciples who make other disciples. Thankfully, we are not alone in this endeavor. We have the Holy Spirit to guide us and correct us when we make mistakes. We have an instruction manual in the Bible and from the experiences of those who have come before us. It's just a matter of maintaining the discipline to continuously learn and advance His Kingdom.

Maintenance

It's impossible to overstate the importance of airplane maintenance. Every time a flight lands, numerous checks are made internally and externally. Even minor issues are addressed so they don't become major problems. Anyone who has flown much has probably spent a few additional minutes on the ground so the maintenance crew could double-check or repair something. As annoying as the delay may be, it's far better to catch something early.

We need maintenance too. Minor issues that are ignored can turn into major problems. Understanding some simple truths and fastidiously applying them to our lives can avert disaster down the line. One of the greatest tools of our spiritual maintenance is understanding the process of sin in our lives. This is critical. Most people don't get it. Some even teach things that hinder people from really growing. But once you see how sin wants to work in your life, you can learn how to keep it out.

Allow me to depart the analogy of flight for a moment to convey this eye-opening truth. Let me introduce you to the hogweed. In the 19th century, botanists from Europe found this magnificent plant in Central Asia and brought its seeds home. They planted it in gardens and cultivated it. The next century, it showed up in North America and it continues to grow wild today in parts of the northern United States and Canada.

The hogweed can top 15 feet in height. Its leaves can span over two feet wide. When it flowers, it can produce an attractive array of white clusters up to four feet wide. As the early botanists noted, it's an impressive specimen. There's only one problem: it can seriously burn or even blind anyone that comes in contact with it.

The sap from the hogweed reacts with the sun to cause burns and blisters on those who touch it. If it gets in your eyes, it can rob you of your sight temporarily or even permanently. The chemicals it produces can even cause cancer and birth defects. Thousands of people across North America and Europe have been caught unaware of its dangers and paid a painful price.

Sin is a lot like the hogweed. Its seed was brought here long ago, some still cultivate it, and many more don't realize the danger until they've already been burned by it. Some become spiritually blinded by it. It often looks impressive or even beautiful, but it's toxic and harmful. The best defense against both sin and the hogweed is, obviously, to avoid contact. But when it is a part of the landscape, it's essential to understand how it grows, what it looks like, and how to deal with it.

James outlines the germination and growth of sin. He says, *"But each one is tempted when he is carried away and enticed by his own lust. Then when lust has conceived, it gives birth to sin; and when sin is accomplished, it brings forth death"* (James 1:14–15).

It starts with "lust," which has a sexual undertone in our times, but simply has the Greek connotation of "desire." This is where sin germinates: with desire. It may be sexual, but can just as easily be emotional, financial, physical, or a number of things. It may be a desire for wealth, a need for the approval of others, a craving for intimacy, and so on. The important thing to note is that it's not yet sin. It's just a seed, not a weed. We all have legitimate desires, and at this point, they are not necessarily sinful.

Once we experience that desire, we are tempted to fulfill it in a number of ways. Where we plant that seed of desire makes all the difference on how it grows. We have legitimate needs, but we can be tempted to meet them in illegitimate ways. This germination primarily occurs with the thoughts in our minds. We either take the thought *"captive to the obedience of Christ,"*[1] which is submission to Him, or we can go in the wrong direction and begin to dwell on it and plot its implementation.

Scripture tells us that Jesus was *"tempted in all things as we are, yet without sin"* (Hebrews 4:15). If Christ was tempted, but did not sin, then there is no inherent sin in temptation. This is critical to understand because many believers think that the mere existence of temptation means they are living in perpetual sin. Men become convinced that the desire to provide for our families is a form of greed or that noticing an attractive woman is sinful lust. Women believe that their anger over a situation automatically makes them a bad person. Children are given the impression that every selfish impulse means they are on the fast track to hell. But the presence of temptation is not sin. Otherwise, Christ would not have been perfect since He was tempted *"in all things."*

Now I know what many of you, especially those raised in the church, are thinking. Jesus said that if you are angry, you are guilty of murder. And that if you lust, you are guilty of adultery. Well, yes and no. Here's that passage:

> *"'You have heard that the ancients were told, "You shall not commit murder" and "Whoever commits murder shall be liable to the court." But I say to you that everyone who is angry with his brother shall be guilty before the court . . . . You have heard that it was said, "You shall not commit adultery"; but I*

---

[1] *2 Corinthians 10:5*

say to you that everyone who looks at a woman with lust for her has already committed adultery with her in his heart.'"

Matthew 5:21–22, 27–28

If you look at that entire chapter, it starts with the Sermon on the Mount where Christ turned the Old Testament law on its ear by declaring such radical ideas as the poor in spirit will inherit the Kingdom of Heaven (as opposed to those who are ultra-religious) and that those who showed mercy would receive mercy (as opposed to those who upheld every punishment proscribed by the law). This drastic departure from traditional teaching was followed by His declaration that *"unless your righteousness surpasses that of the scribes and Pharisees, you will not enter the kingdom of heaven"* (v20).

Jesus then made the statements equating anger with murder and lust with adultery and said that those hidden impulses made one "guilty before the court." He continued by saying that if your eye makes you stumble, you should cut it out and throw it away. Is this really how we should live? If so, then the vast majority of us should be seriously maimed and self-mutilation should be a sign of righteousness. I don't believe Christ was laying down the law, but destroying it.

He goes on to say, "'*Again, you have heard that the ancients were told, "You shall not make false vows, but shall fulfill your vows to the Lord."'"* As in the previous examples, He is quoting Jewish law. But then He directly contradicts it. "'*But I say to you, make no oath at all . . .* '" (v34). Instead of living by the oaths of the ancient laws, He says that we should simply live by an honest "yes" or "no" in our statements. He even goes so far as to say, *"anything beyond these is of evil"* (v37).

That chapter closes with Christ's statement, *"Therefore you are to be perfect, as your heavenly Father is perfect"* (v48). Obviously, we cannot be perfect on our own or under the law, so what is He saying? I believe He was laying down the foundation for the New Covenant – one that is no longer between God and His chosen people, but between the Father and the Son. We cannot be perfect, but, as Paul later wrote, *"We proclaim Him, admonishing every man and teaching every man with all wisdom, so that we may present every man perfect in Christ"* (Colossians 1:28). Technically, the New American Standard Bible says, *". . . complete in Christ."* The King James Version renders it *"perfect."* But the Greek word is *teleios* in both Colossians and in Matthew. Jesus and Paul used the same word to convey "perfection" and "completion." On our own, we are not perfect, nor are we complete. But in Christ, we are made perfect and complete.

So what does this have to do with sin? Let's continue with the process laid out in James' letter. First there is a desire. Then there is the temptation to fulfill it in an ungodly way. Next, he says, *"when lust has conceived, it gives birth to sin"* (James 1:15). The sin is not there until the desire gives in to the temptation. Sin is not *"birthed"* until the lust is *"conceived."* Desire, temptation, conception, sin. When the sin is accomplished, he says, it brings death.

Let's look at this in a common situation. We all have a desire to be treated honestly and fairly. But if someone lies about you, you feel slighted. This is natural. Our desire for truth and justice demands a response. How do you respond? This is the real decision point. You may be tempted to punch the liar in the face. If you dwell on it, you may devise a scheme to really get back at your offender. Maybe slash his tires or tell an even worse lie about him. After all, he deserves it!

At this point, is there sin? According to the law, as Jesus outlined it, you would be *"guilty before the court."* But according to James, the sin has not yet been birthed. You haven't yet punched him or slashed his tires. If you accomplish either of those actions, however, then you have committed the sin. Then you will pay the price, whether it lands you in jail or results in a form of spiritual death. This is how the poisonous weed of sin grows. Desire, temptation, conception, sin, death. Seed, cultivation, growth, poison, pain.

Understanding this process and identifying it when it occurs enables you to abort sin before it is birthed. You're killing the weed before it grows. At the same time, you're freeing yourself from blame that is not from God. Satan is the *"accuser of our brethren"*[2] and he does it non-stop. He tempts you, then accuses you of the sin before you've even accomplished it! We need not live under this cloud of condemnation. Under the law, you would be guilty. But in Christ, you have the gracious room to deal with it first. Then, as Paul stated, *"there is now no condemnation for those who are in Christ Jesus. For the law of the Spirit of life in Christ Jesus has set you free from the law of sin and of death"* (Romans 8:1–2).

We know that temptations will come in this life. I believe they are the "flaming arrows of the evil one" described in Ephesians 10:16. The good news is also found in that passage, which guarantees that those flames will be extinguished with the "shield of faith." When wrong desires tempt us, we must enact our faith by sticking to the truth of God in order to quench them before they go any further.

How many colossal downfalls could have been prevented had the victim extinguished the desire that tempted them before allowing it to be carried out? Sadly, the common logic is, "Well, I've

---
[2] *Revelation 12:10*

already sinned just by having a bad thought, so I'm a sinner and I can't stop it from happening." But that's completely wrong. The point of temptation is the place where we make our stand and decide we will cultivate that hogweed seed so it can sprout and burn us.

Bear in mind that sin has deep roots in this fallen world. If you've seen the movie *Monty Python and the Holy Grail*, you might remember that scene during the bubonic plague where the man pushes a cart through town crying, "Bring out your dead!" Someone attempts to throw out a man who's still alive, claiming he's very ill and near death. The man objects with lines like "I'm getting better" and "I feel happy!" The cart driver has to smack him over the head with a club to shut him up and load him on the cart. Sin will insist it's still alive and well in you, so when it starts kicking, don't let it up. Smack it with the truth of God's Word until it can't move in your life.

We will be tempted. Don't feel guilty for feeling that ungodly desire. Recognize it and deal with it before it is "conceived." That word – *sullambano* in Greek – means to seize and take one as prisoner. A bad thought is not a sin until it seizes you and makes you its captive. So when it occurs, resist it, submit to God, and don't allow it to become sin.

Paul wrote to the believers in Ephesus, *"Be angry, and yet do not sin; do not let the sun go down on your anger . . . "* (Ephesians 4:26). Your anger makes you guilty under the Old Testament law, but we don't live under that law since the death and resurrection of Christ. If you can be angry and still not sin, then the anger is not a sin. Is this an excuse to harbor anger and other negative emotions? Absolutely not. *"Are we to continue in sin so that grace may increase?"* Paul asked. *"May it never be!"*(Romans 6:1–2) he answered. When anger, lust, envy, fear, or any other negative emotion or thought hits your mind, do not sin. Deal with it and submit it to God. That's what it means not to let the sun go down on your anger. You don't cultivate it. You handle it quickly. Then it does not birth sin.

This is spiritual maintenance, to go back to the airplane analogy. Uprooting sin before it grows ensures safe flight. It's a routine process that occurs throughout every day and it's vital to our well-being. Our spiritual health depends on it. Even our very lives may hinge on whether we properly maintain our hearts and minds. So fight the good fight of faith. You can win. That's the promise of the Gospel and the good news we all need.

Inspections

According to the FAA Handbook, "Inspections are visual examinations and manual checks to determine the condition of an aircraft or component. An aircraft inspection can range from a casual walk-around to a detailed inspection involving complete disassembly and the use of complex inspection aids."

When routine maintenance fails to solve a problem, an airplane is grounded for further inspection. It may need to have an engine taken apart and rebuilt. Rivets may need to be replaced. Natural wear-and-tear requires a close look into every part of the aircraft.

We need inspections too. These can range from a quick check of our attitude to a complete dismantling of damaging thought patterns. To use Paul's language, *"Test yourselves to see if you are in the faith; examine yourselves . . . "* (2 Corinthians 13:5).

The FAA handbook also says, "Always use a checklist when performing an inspection." Perhaps the most thorough checklist for us spiritually lies in the passage outlining the fruit of the Spirit.

"But the fruit of the Spirit is love, joy, peace, patience, kindness, goodness, faithfulness, gentleness, self-control; against such things there is no law."

Galatians 5:22–23

If you find these things lacking in your life, you may need to go back to square one and check your beliefs. Paul put this level of urgency on it: *"And if I give all my possessions to feed the poor, and if I surrender my body to be burned, but do not have love, it profits me nothing"* (1 Corinthians 13:3). That's pretty drastic. Most of us haven't given all of our money to feed the poor and I don't know anyone who has surrendered their body to be burned. So it's a little alarming to think one could go to such extreme measures and still have nothing. That's how important love is. And really, the same goes for every other fruit of the Spirit.

Fruit should naturally occur. It shouldn't be a battle. Missing fruit indicates a lack of Holy Spirit control in an area. The most gifted preacher renders himself worthless without kindness. The most generous businessman thwarts his effectiveness if he lacks patience. A champion mother or father wrecks his or her family without faithfulness. You may have an abundance of love and joy, but zero self-control. That's a blatant indicator that something is not functioning properly. You need to ask God (and possibly some Christian friends, leaders, or counselors) what is causing that missing fruit to be stifled. All of these things are necessary because they work in tandem with each other, carrying us to greater heights of Kingdom living. If you aren't producing all of these things, there's a reason. A detailed inspection will help you find the cause.

In addition to missing fruit, another "maintenance light" we sometimes see is rotten fruit. When the fruit of the Spirit is in your life in certain circumstances, but breaks down in other situations, it's not healthy fruit. Loving your friends is easy, but Jesus said to love your enemies. That requires an exceptionally healthy love. If you are patient with people at work or school, but short-tempered at home, there is a malady somewhere. It could be the pain of your past, a byproduct of some bad belief, or another reason that the Holy Spirit is not flowing freely in every area, but there is a source. Find that rottenness and deal with it so healthy fruit will grow.

Finally, fake fruit is not fruit. My wife once bought plastic bananas that looked so real that I picked one up to eat it, only to discover it was phony. We laughed about it, but it's not funny when people put on such a polished exterior that they fool others. Eventually, someone will get close enough to spot the fraud. Joy that relies on circumstances instead of Christ is not real joy. Kindness for the sake of manipulating others is not genuine kindness.

To have an authentic life, we must first be honest with ourselves so we can be honest with others. God is not a God of shame; that's something we put on ourselves when we try to fake it. God wants us to be real. He desires to enable genuine love, joy, peace, and so on. Pretense does not please Him and it benefits us none. Only authentic fruit can provide nourishment and life for others.

If you bear none of the Holy Spirit's fruit, but have an abundance of rotten fruit (like anger, hatred, deception, envy, and such) then it's pretty fair to say that you're not functioning as a believer. Banana trees won't grow pineapples, and if a peach tree grows mangoes, well, it's not a peach tree. We must allow the Holy Spirit to thoroughly work in our lives so we can naturally pour out genuine character.

Safety inspectors are every bit as important as competent pilots. They catch defections and equipment degradation before something causes catastrophic failure. Similarly, spiritual inspections allow us to take inventory of our lives so we can correct things before they go terribly wrong. Use the fruit of the Spirit as a personal checklist and evaluation mechanism to make the necessary changes in your life so you can ensure a better journey.

Chapter 11 ···

PURPOSE

Everyone boards an aircraft with the same goal in mind: arriving at the desired destination. This is the ultimate goal of the journey. If someone wanted to get to Paris, they would not board a plane to Tokyo. As a passenger, that's really all we care about. But as a pilot, there are many other concerns involved. The flight crew can't simply sit back and enjoy the ride. They must plan the route and execute it with real purpose in order to make the trip worthwhile. If the plane left before allowing passengers to board or flew around South America to get from New York to San Francisco, we would call them lousy pilots.

When navigating through life, understanding why we are traveling, how long it will take to get there, and where the ride will take us only makes sense.

Objective

The point of boarding a flight is pretty obvious. You want to get somewhere specific. Yet many people seem to miss the point of the

Christian life. Certainly it is to get to Heaven, but there has to be more to it than that or we'd have no point in living. Someday, all believers will enter the Kingdom of Heaven, but on this journey we must bring a measure of Heaven to this earth.

"As you go, preach, saying, 'The kingdom of heaven is at hand'" (Matthew 10:7) Jesus declared. He didn't use the future tense, He meant here and now. As we share His love, make disciples, and shine His truth in this dark world, we do so with a sense of purpose that stems from the entirety of the Scripture and God's deliberately-crafted plan to restore mankind to Himself.

In Isaiah 58, the prophet pointed to a day when God's people would move beyond religious observation of the law and into a day of real glory. I believe he's talking about the day of Christ. In that passage, Isaiah says that God's people will be a *"well watered garden"* (v11) and *"like a spring of water whose waters do not fail"* (v11). What a beautiful picture! Gardens provide nutrition and a place to rest. Springs provide life-giving water to drink and refresh those who are weary.

Here's an interesting thing about a well-watered garden. It receives water, but then it drains. It doesn't hold the water to itself. It flows out. A garden that doesn't release water is a swamp. Have you ever smelled a swamp? It's stagnant and unfruitful. The Dead Sea gets its name from the fact that not much can live in it. Why? Because though the Jordan River flows into it and a few natural springs feed it, there is no outflow. The result is a salinity that's eight times saltier than the ocean. You can make embalming fluid from it, but you can't get much life out of it!

This is the danger of receiving God's grace, but never releasing it. We can become spiritual Dead Seas. Paul stipulated the other side of grace; that is, he declares what the outcome of God's grace in our lives should be:

> "For by grace you have been saved through faith; and that not of yourselves, it is the gift of God; not as a result of works, so that no one may boast. For we are His workmanship, created in Christ Jesus for good works, which God prepared beforehand so that we would walk in them."
>
> Ephesians 2:8–10

This is God's order of things: grace, faith, salvation, good works. God's grace comes through Christ. Our faith in Him brings salvation. We then have the power to do good works, which extends God's grace to others. This is the crux of my message in this book. His grace is here; accept it. Grow strong in your faith in Christ. Rejoice in the assurance of your salvation. Begin to do good works so that His grace can flow out of your life and into others. That's soaring. That's rising above.

Given that this is His truth, it's no wonder that Satan, who distorts all truth, attempts to convince people that good works are the prerequisite to salvation, proving our faith and somehow earning God's grace. But that's exactly backwards! If that's how you live your life, you will not effectively share His grace with others because you are focused on earning or proving your own salvation. But once you have faith in Christ, that is settled.

When you think about it, how can anyone sustain a lifetime of good works apart from God's grace? Trying to "be good" without knowing the One who is the very essence of goodness is like trying to write the great American novel without any knowledge of the English language. It's an endeavor destined to fail. But once we possess saving faith through the gracious gift of Jesus Christ, we can move on in our journey. To really live the life God has planned for you, you must understand the order of things so you can focus your energy in the right direction. Your objective is to share His grace as you "walk" in good works.

Walking, in the context of Paul's native language, has several connotations – none of which have to do with literal walking. The first is "to conduct one's self." That's the natural inference of "walking in good works." It means you do them. The good news is that when faith genuinely transforms your heart and mind, you don't have to strive to conduct yourself in good works. That's what God remade you to do – just do them! Walking and conducting are actions. You don't complete your God-given mission in life by thinking about it; you complete it by doing it.

Another connotation of "walking" is "progressing." On long flights, time moves slowly and progress seems to creep along, even though you're travelling at hundreds of miles per hour. Walking in the Spirit can feel that way. It's hard to see in the daily grind. Learning to inject spiritual growth into otherwise mundane activities helps provide a sense of progress. More importantly, it prepares you for times when there's a more urgent need for an active, tangible faith.

Singing along with praise music on the drive to work, silently praying for others throughout the day, offering modestly encouraging words to others during casual contact, meditating on Scripture as you go to sleep, and other simple actions can keep you moving in the right direction. That's progress. If you're just starting out, don't worry about being inconsistent or ineffective, you will improve; don't lose heart, just keep doing them with the faith that His Word is true. It will have an impact. Guaranteed.

Walking also means "making use of opportunities." We all have opportunities for good works if we will just have the awareness to see them. You don't have to quit your job, move to another country, and become a full-time missionary to make use of opportunities. You just have to notice that co-worker who's having a difficult time, befriend that lonely student, or provide for the needy in your community. In reality, you cannot avoid opportunities to do good works. You just need to make use of them.

My friend Matthew Barnett exemplifies this truth. When he was only 20 years old he moved from his father's church in Phoenix to Los Angeles' inner city, right on the Hollywood Freeway, to minister at a hospital converted to "The Dream Center." After two years of frustration and failure trying to execute the plan he had in mind, God called him to lay down all of his dreams to partake in His dream to "love, serve, and give what you have away."[1] He embarked on a decades-long mission to reach gang members, homeless families, drug addicts, and other spiritually dying people. He did that simply by making use of the opportunities around him. "Once you start meeting needs," Matthew told me, "you start discovering all these visions in your life that you never knew you had." Those visions are God's visions. We just need to take hold of them.

Christians have a language they speak (for better or worse) that can often lose meaning when used as a catchphrase. "Putting your faith in action" is one such phrase, though it is rooted in Scripture. It simply means to act like you believe it. Are you no longer dead in sin? Then act like it! Are you alive in Jesus Christ? Then act like it! Having received the grace of salvation, does God now have good works for you to do? Then do them!

....
[1] *http://youtu.be/D_0hJ-wpHYs*

This is the purpose of God's grace. It flows into your life, makes all things new, and bears fruit. Then it's ready to flow out of you to others. It's a continuous process. If you don't receive the gracious gifts of God daily (peace, wisdom, love, discernment, and so on) then you will become a desert. If you don't release them, you will become a swamp. Neither is God's design. You are to be a river of life, first receiving from God, then pouring out to others.[2] This is your objective. This is the reason you are on this earth. Before you arrive at your eternal destination, this is the point of your life.

Duration

I'm the guy that checks his watch on takeoff so I can calculate our arrival. On those long flights with the map of the flight path, elapsed time, and arrival time, I leave the TV monitor on that channel so I can watch our progress. Whether the flight is short or long, I'm all about the duration.

Jesus' brother, James, wrote, *"Yet you do not know what your life will be like tomorrow. You are just a vapor that appears for a little while and then vanishes away. Instead, you ought to say, 'If the Lord wills, we will live and also do this or that'"* (James 4:14–15).

We don't know how long this journey will last. For some, it seems tragically short. Others live well beyond the average life expectancy. What we do know is that we are to make the most of our time. However many years we spend on this earth, we must endure in our faith to the end.

Paul describes life as a race – more of a marathon than a sprint. To a runner, that means pace and endurance. It means not worrying about those in front or behind, but focusing on the road

---

[2] *John 7:38–39*

ahead and never quitting. Scriptures often refer to endurance in the context of persecution, and you may face maltreatment to some degree, but it also speaks of endurance in two other areas you will certainly face.

The first is in our faith. Our faith will be tested. James also wrote " . . . *the testing of your faith produces endurance*" (James 1:3). We must be determined to believe God's truth no matter what life throws at us. This is easier said than done. I have interviewed parents who have lost a child, couples whose marriage has been rocked by infidelity, and missionaries who have faced horrific circumstances. Despite their devastation, their faith endured.

I would venture to say that we will all encounter something that could tempt us to lose our faith in God. That's why it's so critical that we start by truly believing. Nobody in their right mind would fly a structurally weak airplane into a storm, yet people often think nothing of taking weak faith into the storms of life. Naturally, it fractures when tested.

Paul told Timothy, *"If we endure, we will also reign with Him; If we deny Him, He also will deny us . . . "* (2 Timothy 2:12). The first part of that is not just a poetic expression; it's a promise. The latter half is a warning. So when you hit that faith-shattering turbulence, remember the promise. And if you deny Christ during the difficult times, don't be surprised with the results. The best plan in those crisis moments is to run quickly into the presence of God and hold fast to this promise: those who endure will *reign* with Jesus Christ. Cling to that truth and you will be able to endure every devastating circumstance in life. Every single one.

The other area in which we must exercise endurance is in love. Love *"bears all things, believes all things, hopes all things, endures all things"* (1 Corinthians 13:7). Again, this is easier said than done.

People do things, whether incidentally or purposely, to give us ample reason not to love them. That's why our love for others must not come from others; it must come from God. Take a moment to consider that truth. Do you love someone because they please you or do you love because you are called to love? Think of the person you dislike the most. Now consider the truth that Jesus Christ died for him or her and desires a relationship with that person. You, as a believer, are a conduit for His love. The love you show that individual cannot be contingent upon reciprocation. No matter what he or she does, the love of God, through you, must endure.

If you can begin to look *through* people to see Christ at work in them, you gain a better perspective on love. It's easy to love our friends, but Jesus told us to love our enemies.[3] Don't expect them to love you back. Your love is not predicated on others. Instead, it's a mark of who you are. *"By this all men will know that you are My disciples, if you have love for one another"* (John 13:35). Redefining your motivation for loving others vastly increases your ability to love.

Enduring in things like faith, hope, love, and the other Godly characteristics energizes, empowers, and enables us to make it through to the end, with the hope of one day hearing the Lord say, "Well done."

Mission

We are not on a pleasure flight; we are on a rescue mission. This is not the party charter to Vegas. It's more like the firefighter planes used to thwart raging wildfires or the seaplanes used to pluck people from the ocean. Our task is not to soar merely for our own benefit, but to share the glorious life we have been given with

....
[3] *Matthew 5:44*

others we come in contact with. We do this through those "good deeds" for which we were created.

Once you understand that works are not the condition for salvation, but the natural outflow of genuine faith, you can see why it's not legalistic to say, *"For just as the body without the spirit is dead, so also faith without works is dead"* (James 2:26). You don't perform works to revive a dead spirit; instead, a faith that is alive can't stop doing good things. Jesus didn't scold Lazarus for just laying there in the tomb. He raised him from the dead! When we are called by Christ to rise up and do something, we have the power to obey. Until then, we're incapable of doing much.

So what constitutes "good deeds" in God's eyes? Ultimately, there is only one thing: doing His will. Certainly, there are many good actions that occur between people. Volunteering for a cause helps people, and they are grateful. Doing your job well is a good work to your boss, and for that, you are paid. Giving to a charity will usually get you a tax write-off. But there is no good deed that accrues heavenly wealth outside of those things that are performed in direct obedience to Him.

The Pharisees performed many good works, even to the point of tediously obeying the law. Still, Jesus quoted Isaiah to them, saying, ""*. . . This people honors Me with their lips, but their heart is far away from Me*"" (Mark 7:6).

This goes to the core of our motives. Works intended to secure salvation are essentially selfish. If we could earn our way to Heaven, who wouldn't want to? Life would be a grand contest of charity with the winner taking the highest pedestal in Heaven forever. Whoever came in last would surely feel eternal shame! But since it's through grace we are saved, nobody can brag about themselves.[4] Even those rewards we receive will be laid down at the feet of the One whose accomplishments make the rest of ours seem insignificant in comparison.[5]

The current fad with causes, though certainly pursuing good ends, are merely self-satisfying endeavors apart from the leadership of God. In 2008, the BBC reported a Canadian scientific study that proved it. The headline read: *"Charity 'Makes You Feel Better.'"* A psychologist claimed to have proof that "charitable giving improved how people saw themselves."[6] Of course, giving to others helps the recipients in most cases, but when we go to the motive, there is still an element of self that tarnishes any altruism.

It could then be said that only believers can truly perform good works, since unbelievers do so without any guidance from Christ. While we acknowledge that in man's view, any word or action that helps others carries a level of human goodness, can we really claim that we possess true goodness on our own in the eyes of God? St. Augustine said, in *The City of God*, "Good works, as they are called, in sinners, are nothing but splendid sins." Solomon, in his diary of wisdom, declared man's existence *"vanity of vanities"* (Ecclesiastes 2:8). We must derive our motivation from One greater than us in order to ascend to the level of goodness in His eyes.

Remember, Jesus Christ is the vine and we are the branches.[7] Any fruit that grows out of the nourishment provided by the sap from the vine is of God. Anything else is not. It may be a good deed in the eyes of man, but without divine inspiration, it is not a

....
[4] *1 Corinthians 1:31*
[5] *Revelation 4:9–11*
[6] *http://news.bbc.co.uk/2/hi/health/7305395.stm*
[7] *John 15:5*

good deed in the eyes of God. People may do worthwhile acts to improve the lives of others, but it is done with an inferior motive unless it is done in direct obedience to Him. While such actions may have a temporary benefit, they will not have an eternal reward.

Consider the man who leaves his home to work in a developing country. Perhaps he spends years in the most remote parts of Africa teaching the poor how to farm. He would, no doubt, save lives. He would at least bring survival skills to those in desperate need. But if that man has done so against the wishes of his wife and neglected his own children, has he really done a good work? Probably not. Unless a work is inspired of God, bringing glory to Him above all else, and carried out in obedience to the Holy Spirit, it does not matter how wonderful others claim it is or how beneficial it may be to society, it is not a "good work" because it is not a "God work." Our words and actions are only good deeds when God leads. To rise to the level of divine, they must be ordained by God, empowered by His Spirit, and bring glory to Him.

Chapter 12

ARRIVAL

I landed in Nashville to an excited crowd. It was obvious by their banners that they weren't there for me, but rather some soldiers returning from the Middle East. I noticed the soldiers on my flight – dozens of men and women in military fatigues – but I didn't realize until disembarking that they had been away for many months and were just about to be reunited with their families. No doubt they had been on many flights since leaving home, but this one from DFW to Nashville was special because of the reward awaiting them on the ground.

So what's the payoff for believers, both now and for eternity? There are several. Some we will see in this lifetime and some we will experience after death. There are many and they vary for each individual, but some apply to all of us. Of course, the journey itself is a reward. Life as a friend of the Most High God should be glorious – and it is. Compared to the pain those who live separated from God feel, even the most difficult trials with Him become bearable.

His burden is easy and His yoke is light.[1] There are innumerable rewards, but a few that I want to explore here.

Rewards

The primary reward for flight lies in the speed with which one can change locations. I have literally had breakfast in Rwanda, lunch in London, and dinner in Texas all in the same long day. In a relatively short time, one can go across the country or around the world. The scenery can go from cold to warm, mountainous to tropical, and domestic to foreign. It's an amazing transformation of landscape and culture.

When we begin to walk in the Spirit every day, things can change rapidly. Our words and actions can go from bringing death to bringing life immediately. Our perspective changes, making our outlook completely different. A negative past can be rendered powerless, and a promising future can become reality. The rewards of soaring higher in Christ and going further in His plan are almost limitless. But it doesn't stop there.

A Spirit-filled life can also impact those around us in profound and eternal ways. Perhaps the most underrated aspect of the power of God is the innate ability to change the minds and hearts of people. Paul said, *"We are destroying speculations and every lofty thing raised up against the knowledge of God . . . "* (2 Corinthians 10:5). The world attempts to change people's minds by appealing to selfish, fleshly desires. Advertisers persuade and often lie about their products to get your money. Politicians tickle your ears to get your vote. People flatter, pretend, and manipulate in order to gain your affection, confidence, or support. But the goal of the Godly

....
[1] *Matthew 11:30*

ability to change people's minds is not self-serving, it's redemptive. Contrary to the worldly purpose of influence, the point of Paul's concept is that inspiring Godly ideas in the minds of others helps them more than it helps us. By tearing down the ideas that stand in opposition to God, we are able to raise those that are of Him. And it always gives glory to God, not ourselves.

Since salvation comes through belief, we must work to change the way people think. We must shake their false beliefs and give them the truth of the Gospel. We cannot force people to believe it – that is the integrity of free will – but we can present it in a way that will influence the most people. Jesus said before His crucifixion, *"And I, if I am lifted up from the earth, will draw all men to Myself'"* (John 12:32). The greatest argument for Christ is not necessarily the one we form with our words, but the one we shape with our lives.

We learn to soar for this reason. We lift Jesus Christ up with our words and deeds by living a life that is consistent, stable, bold, and redemptive. We show the world a better way to live and invite them to partake in it. Paul wrote, *"Be imitators of me, just as I also am of Christ"* (1 Corinthians 11:1). That doesn't mean we don a tunic and sandals, abstain from marriage, bear no children, and die at the hands of Roman soldiers. It means we look to God in every aspect of our lives. We follow as the Holy Spirit leads.

This world is steeped in darkness; yet we are of the Light. We must be bold in confronting the spirits and attitudes that prevail. The first-century church knew this. Luke wrote, *" . . . they were all filled with the Holy Spirit and began to speak the word of God with boldness"* (Acts 4:31). The Bible overflows with stories of those who bravely stood against the evil of their time. We can and must do the same. As we tear down the ideas that stand in defiance of God, we can see His Spirit move in the lives of others.

By living in the experiential life of a Christ follower, you gain the knowledge, wisdom, and discernment to be *"ready to make a defense to everyone who asks you to give an account for the hope that is in you"* (1 Peter 3:15). The early believers lived a life so clearly marked by God's presence that people often asked them, "What must I do to be saved?" When the Holy Spirit resides in us with such power that others notice, we will have the opportunity to reveal the reason we are radically different and share the truth with them. We can make disciples and expand the Kingdom of God. This is perhaps one of the most rewarding aspects of our journey. We are changed, and therefore, we inspire change in others.

Reunion

Just as those soldiers were reunited with their families in that Nashville airport, believers can look forward to reuniting with loved ones who are also believers. Those of us who have lost loved ones understand the comfort in this truth. When my sister passed away, I genuinely felt like she had simply relocated to another place – one that I will eventually move to as well. Though there is sorrow in seeing anyone leave, we do not mourn without hope.[2] If we truly believe His Word, we should think and act as if this life is merely a staging ground for eternity. It's not the destination, it's the terminal. Flights depart every day, and we all have an assigned seat on one to come.

Frankly, the issue I struggle with the most is trying to comfort those who have lost loved ones who did not know Christ. I sincerely hope that God has a hidden plan to bring everyone to Him eventually, but I don't believe the Scripture supports any form of

....
[2] *1 Thessalonians 4:13*

universalism. To the contrary, I see a God who desires that none should perish, but allows each individual to make that choice. That's why there's such urgency in sharing the Gospel.

World War II films and documentaries fascinate me. When the Allies invaded on D-Day, the skies were filled with c-47s and other massive aircrafts dropping thousands of paratroopers. So many of those planes were hit by flak and enemy fire that men were often scrambling to get out the door before their carrier went down. That's the urgency we should feel for the lost. This world has been assaulted by the enemy, but we have a parachute of grace. We just need to get to the only door that leads to life, and that is Jesus Christ.

Things are chaotic here. A spiritual battle rages. But the final outcome is a foregone conclusion. The victory has already been won. The V-Day celebration will be momentous. John got a glimpse of what is to come and recorded it in the book of Revelation:

> *"'Behold, the tabernacle of God is among men, and He will dwell among them, and they shall be His people, and God Himself will be among them, and He will wipe away every tear from their eyes; and there will no longer be any death; there will no longer be any mourning, or crying, or pain; the first things have passed away.'"*
>
> Revelation 21:3–4

The tabernacle was the place in the Old Testament where God's presence resided. The promise here is that believers will live in His presence forever. No pain, no sorrow, no death. Just the mind-blowing experience of Almighty God for eternity. When this truth becomes real in our hearts and minds, the losses of this life pale in comparison to the amazing reunion we will have with fellow believers and our awesome Savior. It is a paradise better than any vacation we can imagine on this earth. (For my wife, that means more beautiful that an infinite, pristine beach of smooth sand. For me, that means an endless run of perfect white powder on a crisp winter day. I don't know how God will reconcile the two, but I know it will be better than either of us can imagine!)

I am, of course, getting ahead of myself. While we draw hope and inspiration from things to come, we must focus on the task at hand. We must love those we are with now. We must reach those around us today. The promise of an amazing future should inspire us to grip the present with more purpose, confidence, and power.

I believe God gives us a sneak peek into eternity so we can see this life with a healthier perspective, knowing that the difficulties we face are only temporary. At the same time, I suspect He holds back quite a bit so we don't get too excited to leave. We must never forget that we are here for a reason. Our eventual reunion with those who have moved on will be even sweeter when we carry out the Great Commission and bring more people to the celebration.

Ready For Takeoff

Dreaming about flying is not the same as actually flying. Reading about the process will help prepare you for flight, but it won't get you off the ground. Operating flight simulators provides good training, but when you step out of the simulator, you are in the exact same place that you started! The only way you will ever enjoy the journey and arrive at your destination is to take off. It's time to do the things that will get you there. Consider this your final boarding call.

As you believe in Christ, die to sin, self, and the law, rise up as a new creature, develop the characteristics of a Christ follower, produce the fruit of the Spirit, and soar in the power of one who is led every day by the Holy Spirit, you will not simply know in your mind the truth of God, you will live it. Lay down your pride, set aside the fear, and embark on this glorious journey.

Your faith will be tested. Clever people will try to sway you. Bad things will happen to good people. Your emotions will wage war against the truth. To rise above the atmosphere of this world, you must continually grow in the faith.

Your flesh wants to creep back to life. Paul said to make your life a *"living sacrifice."*(Romans 12:1). My pastor points out that the problem with living sacrifices is that they keep crawling off the altar. It's up to us to put our fleshly desires back in their place.

Character can be eroded and fruit can rot. You must maintain your Godly characteristics and perform routine inspections to prevent the decay of the world from setting in.

You must progress every day. You have been given gifts by God and *"each of us is to exercise them"* (Romans 12:6). Life is a journey, not a campground. New experiences await you. If you're too comfortable or set in your ways, it's time to move. In order to soar, you must leave the tarmac.

What is the impact that this kind of life will have? It's revolutionary. It's greater than any force on earth – greater than any religious organization, political party, or social movement. The day of the timid church that keeps its religious beliefs to itself is over. Jesus Christ has empowered His bride to courageously declare His truth to the world, and you are a part of that declaration.

The Gospel is not merely a comforting balm for superstitious people. It is the only way out of the fire that is consuming those who are dead in sin, both now and for eternity. Believers can no longer sit politely by and say, "Here's the cure for your terminal disease, if you'd like it." We must aggressively go after those dying in their sin and rescue them. We must break down the doors of deception and show people the truth. We must not simply argue against the ideas that stand in the way of the knowledge of God, we must *destroy* them – batter, crush, and obliterate them. This is not a passive concept. This is a very aggressive move against ungodly ideas.

Simultaneously, we must demonstrate love toward those who hold to these poisonous ideas. It's a bit of a paradox – destroying the ideas of someone while imparting life to them – but it is precisely what we are called to do. It's like an antibiotic that kills deadly bacteria in order to bring life to the patient.

As with us, the change in others starts with what they believe. That means influencing them in their very thought process. We cannot do this alone. Clever arguments will not suffice. Manipulation is the wrong way to do it. We are called as witnesses, not lawyers or puppeteers. We tell people what we have genuinely experienced and pray the Holy Spirit will draw them to the point of salvation.

Part of the problem with the modern church is that we haven't witnessed anything to talk about. We can't tell others of God's power because we haven't experienced it ourselves. We cannot give an account for a hope we do not possess. That's why this whole process of believing, dying, rising, and soaring is so critical. We can't expect anyone else to follow in our steps when we haven't walked it ourselves. But when we've undergone a real change and seen the glory of God in our own lives, we are excited to share this with others and eager for them to experience it themselves. This is real witnessing. It's not some painful, begrudging exercise in scaring people about the reality of hell. It's relating the kindness of God in our own lives that led us to repentance and inviting others to get in on the benefits.

This is the essence of spiritual warfare. It's not some mumbo-jumbo incantation or intangible analogy. It's destroying the ideas that set themselves up against God. It's breaking down the strongholds in people's lives that prevent them from intimately knowing Jesus Christ as the Savior. All of those weird rituals and incomprehensible traditions of religion is garbage. Christianity is all about believing in Jesus Christ, following His lead, and sharing His blessings with others. The rest is a distraction of the enemy.

If you want to make your faith really fly as you fulfill your God-given mission in life, focus on that simple truth and ignore the rest. Nobody else can do it for you, and only you can do exactly what God desires in your life. You are called for a purpose, and this is it. He will show you how to carry it out. Experience His grace, grow in His character, and impart that grace to others. This is how you rise above a boring, mediocre faith. You can do it every day . . . starting today.